Colleen Cassir

P9-CJM-000

July 1982
Convergence

Seattle

THE FIBERARTS DESIGN BOOK

FROM THE EDITORS OF FIBERARTS MAGAZINE

FIBERARTS, ASHEVILLE, NORTH CAROLINA
HASTINGS HOUSE PUBLISHERS, NEW YORK, NEW YORK

Cover: Detail of EFFUSIONS by Karen Chapnick

ISBN - 0-937274-00-3 Hardcover
ISBN - 0-937274-01-1 Softcover
Library of Congress Catalog Card No.: 80-67315
Revised Second Printing

Copyright ©1980 by FIBERARTS

Published in 1980 by:
FIBERARTS
P.O. Box 2775
Asheville, North Carolina 28801

Distributed in the United States and Canada by:
HASTINGS HOUSE PUBLISHERS
10 East 40th Street
New York, New York 10016

All rights reserved. No part of this work covered by the copyright hereon may be reproduced or used in any form or by any means—graphic, electronic, or mechanical including photocopying, recording, taping or information storage and retrieval systems—without written permission of the publisher.

The artists contributing to The FIBERARTS Design Book retain copyrights on their individual works presented in this volume.

Printed in the United States of America by:
The Ovid Bell Press, Inc., Fulton, Missouri
Paper: Warren Flokote Gloss 70 lb.
Typeface: Andover 8 pt.

CONTENTS

INTRODUCTION

When this book hits the streets, FIBERARTS Magazine will be just about ready to uncork a few bottles of champagne and start celebrating an important birthday. For the past five years, we've been chronicling the fiber arts, reviewing shows, interviewing artists, and sharing our excitement with our readers.

Now, feet up on the desk, typewriters unplugged and covered for the day, we'll be able to lean back and review our own private memories of those years, and flip through The FIBERARTS Design Book.

It is our latest and most extensive attempt to document the fiber arts, to provide a look at the current trends, and a glimpse at the variety and quality of work being done today in fibers. With it, we hoped to pull from the woodwork, pry from the dark corners, those artists hidden from view, the wallflowers that, so far, have gone unnoticed.

To those of you out there who associate "fiber art" with all those macrame plant hangers that your neighbor's kid keeps making, this book will open wide the doors upon a world that's been around since the early 50's.

During the last thirty years, the conventional wisdom—that painting and sculpture are the only true "fine arts"—began to be challenged. The skills of previous generations were re-discovered, and employed in new and exciting ways. Weaving, crochet, knitting, quilting, stitchery, and more recently, basketry, netting and papermaking, came to be called the fiber arts.

By the late 60's, they were flourishing. Museums were regularly featuring special exhibitions of fiber. New art galleries were cropping up, dealing exclusively with these media, and universities began offering undergraduate and graduate programs in the fiber arts.

To document the emergence of fiber as a new art medium, a free, two-page newsletter was sent out to Southwestern fiber artists in 1974. As the mailing list grew, readers began helping out with the costs of printing and distribution. By January of 1976, the newsletter had evolved into a full-fledged magazine. Today, FIBERARTS is published every two months, and enjoys an international audience of over 50,000.

Curiosity about what the folks in that audience were doing, and a desire to freeze a moment in time, spawned the idea for The FIBERARTS Design Book. It sounded so easy in the beginning—just invite our readers to send in photos and slides of the best work they had done in the last three years, pick out the best, and put them all in a book.

Nice and simple. No late nights. We won't even have to miss the Sunday afternoon volleyball games. It's a good thing that hindsight comes after the fact—otherwise, projects like this would never get out of the "great ideas" file.

As it happened, our optimistic naivete led us to put out a call in the magazine for Design Book entries. At first, they only trickled in . . . just long enough to make the sweat break out on our brows. We began to wonder if we'd have enough to make a book, let alone a GOOD book.

It wasn't too much later that the trickle turned into a deluge.

Mr. Cowan, our friendly postman, and a fine Southern gentleman, suddenly began dragging in first one, and then two, mail-bags a day, full of Design Book entries. And on a couple of Monday mornings, right near

the entry deadline, he actually hauled up three bags that overflowed onto the office floor.

After a month of cataloging the contents of each envelope, we had more than 12,000 slides and photographs from 1300 artists. What followed was a descent into the maelstrom.

The week of courteous debate and selection that we had originally envisioned, stretched into six. In sporadic bursts, sandwiched between deadlines for the magazine, five of us sat in a dark, very hot, smoke-filled room, exploring the nuances of compromise. Universal agreement among us was a rare occurrence and tempers often flared.

Ironically, this wide divergence of opinion resulted in a much more eclectic collection of fiber art than a panel of like-minded judges might have put together. As each of our individual viewpoints were challenged, we began to take a second look at works that we might otherwise have passed by.

We went through 131 slide trays and a file drawer of photographs, using a "yes", "no", "maybe" system of selection. Some entries were reviewed up to half a dozen times before the final decision was made.

Finally, right on the verge of chucking the whole thing and going into auto mechanics, we finished. We had our book. All we had to do was put it together . . . which of course, DID require late nights, weekends and skipping the Sunday volleyball games.

Three basic considerations governed our selections for this book: aesthetic appeal, technical expertise and innovative ideas. The judging process was admittedly subjective, but that's what made it so exciting.

We were surprised to find that hundreds of artists have turned to quilting as a means of expression. Much of our not-so-temperate debate went on while one quilt or another "hung" on our slide screen, because so many of them were outstanding.

We were also impressed with the vitality of contemporary tapestry, and fascinated by the wide ranging experimentation in the area of surface design—using dyes or photographic and Xerox transfer processes on fabric and handmade paper.

Over all, we were drawn to simple, straightforward works, and found ourselves rejecting the cluttered and bulky pieces that characterized the fiber art of the 60's and early 70's.

Having settled on about 500 pieces, we started the grand shuffle, trying to organize everything into coherent chapters. After a lot of fancy footwork and talk about listing them by technique versus subject matter, we settled on a combination.

You'll find some chapters that deal with technique—Surface Design, and Stitched Pressed and Pieced (including needlepoint, handmade paper and quilts). The other works are grouped roughly by form or function—Two Dimensions, Three Dimensions, Miniatures and Wearables. Of course, there are always those unique items that defy classification, and you'll find many of them in Diversions.

So, welcome to our world. Meander on through The FIBERARTS Design Book and discover the reason why we have so much fun putting out a new issue of the magazine every other month!

To all you artists who contributed to this project, whether or not your work is in this book, we uncork another bottle of champagne and salute you. This is YOUR book!

The Editors at FIBERARTS
Asheville, North Carolina
August, 1980

TWO
DIMENSIONS

A

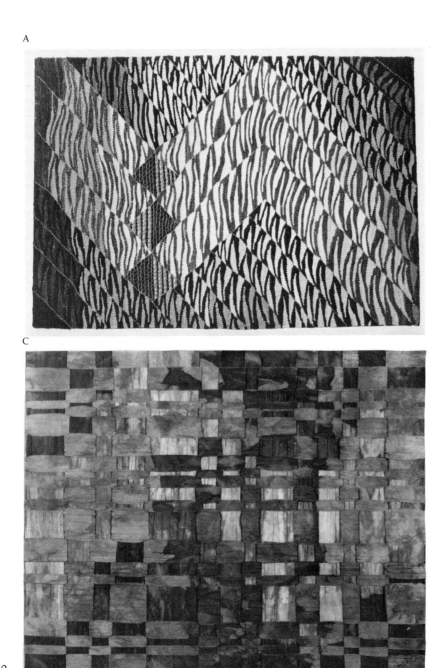

A

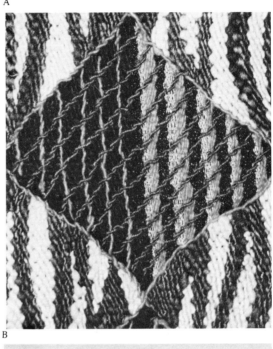

B

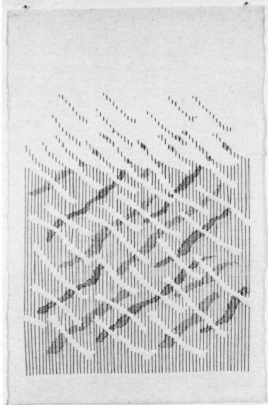

C

D
Shirley E. Held
PILLAR OF LIGHT
Brocade weaving pattern
of cotton and rayon; 15
by 45 inches.

*Because I am a full-time
university professor, my
weaving time is limited—much
of that time is spent
experimenting with color and
transparency.*

E
Alexandra Jacopetti
WHICH PATH TO HEAVEN
Stuffed warp face
weave with weft face
areas; 3 by 5 feet.

F
Elizabeth Nettleton
HOMAGE TO KLEE
Wool and cotton
tapestry; 84 by 114
inches.

D

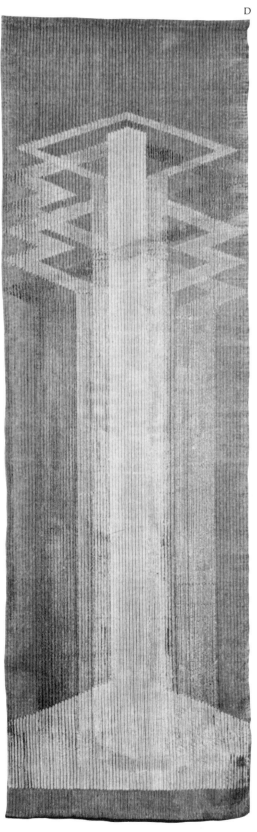

E

F

A
Margrit Schmidtke
AMISH MOON
Mexican tapestry of
handspun New Zealand
fleece (twill threading); 3
by 7 feet.

B
Libby Kowalski
UNTITLED
Double cloth tabby
weave with cotton; 33 by
74 inches.
*I wish my work to emanate a
feeling of strength—to allude
to a higher level of
consciousness. Through my
background in science and
accounting, I have chosen for
my mode of expression an
overall field of patterning with
computer references.*

C
Pam Patrie
FUJI FUJI
French tapestry variation
with wool and cotton; 6
by 4 feet.

A

B

C

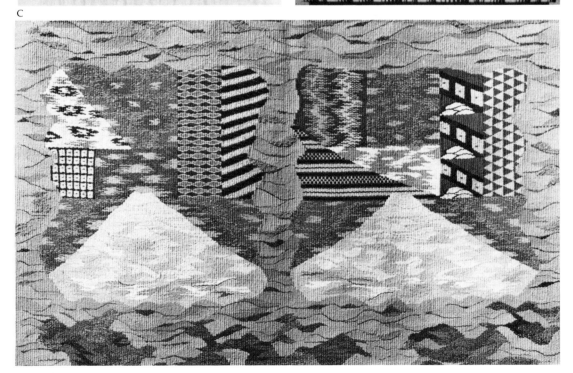

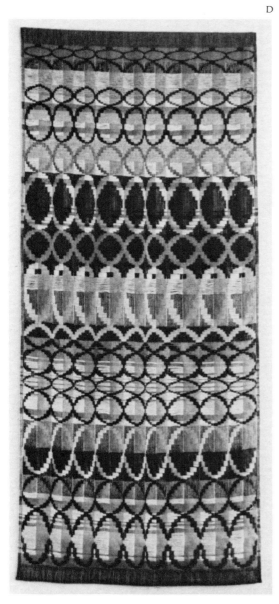

D

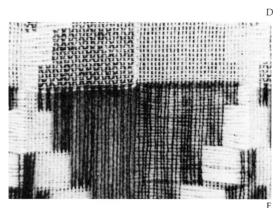

D
Laura J. Strychalski
FASCINATING RHYTHM
Ten-harness brocade of
linen and acrylic; 35 by
78 inches.
*The two concepts which
characterize my work are
structure and movement. I see
each weaving as three-
dimensional, with multiple
layers of intersecting yarns and
cloth. I conceive of my
materials as being alive and in
motion while I work with
them: traveling or dancing,
meeting, chasing or passing
each other.*

E
Karin Lusnak
RUG
Wedge weave (Navajo
pulled warp) of wool and
mohair; 35 by 48 inches.

E

F
Patti Mitchem
GRAY QUARTET
Perle cotton; warp rep
weave; 8 by 4 feet.
*This group gives me the
feeling of a gathering storm.*

F

A
Charlotte Cain
BROOKS BROTHERS #2
Machine knit wool,
pieced and laminated to
cotton canvas; 42 by 76½
inches.

*Underlying all nature is an
infinite field of pure creative
intelligence. Pattern is my
method of articulating my own
experience of this field.*

B
Eileen Vassos-Moffett
SOQUETE VILLA
Cavandoli knotting with
jute; 30 by 62 inches
(including fringe).

*Moving from the East to the
Southwest was an experience
which crystalized my often
disjointed interests. Natural
fiber and earth-tone colors
provide a medium through
which I can capture a whisper
of the enchantment that is
New Mexico.*

A

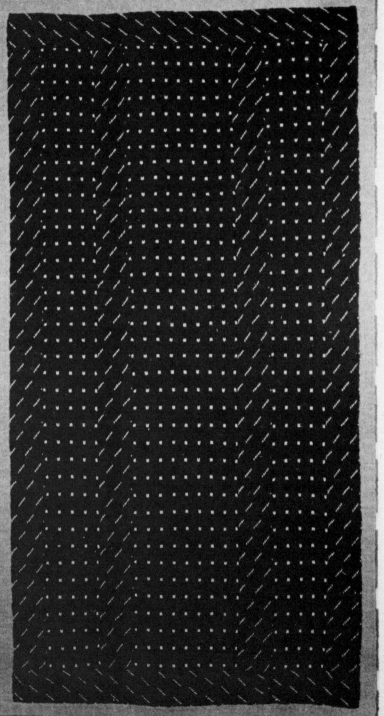

B

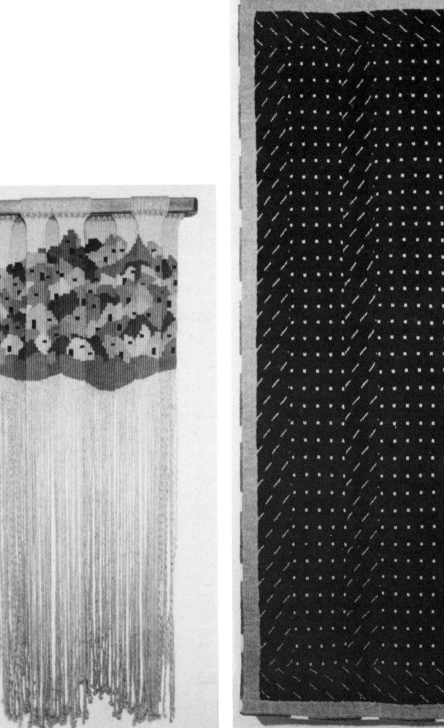

14

C
Barbara Nelson
TRANSPOSITION
Weaving and wrapping with jute, linen, wool and silver floss; 5 by 5 feet.

In order to be able to explore my ideas more fully, I choose to set limits to work within. The square format establishes for me a protected environment within which images of my life experience are reflected.

D
Margaret B. Windeknecht
LAUGHTER II
16-harness loom-controlled weaving of wool and linen; 82 by 34 inches.

Laughter is the universal language. I worked to capture not only the sound of laughter but the aura as well. In each row, a primary color is coupled with its opposite secondary color to create a push-pull so that the total color effect is that of joyful laughter.

E
Susan Iverson
NOTES - V - I
Wool on linen warp, pulled warp tapestry; 78 by 75 inches.

I consider my work to be formal compositions with an initial reference to the viewing of urban architectural structures and/or spaces.

C

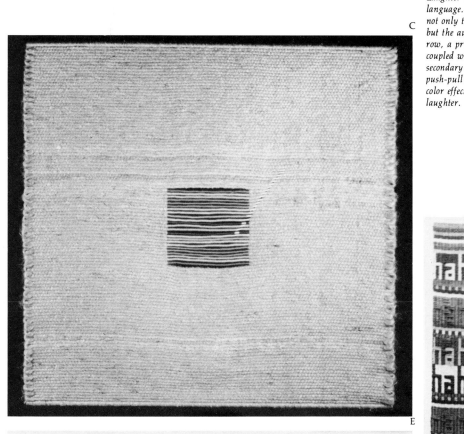

D

E

15

A

Jana Vander Lee

DOWN BY THE BANKS OF
LAUGHING WATER
Linen and polyester
warp; silk, wool, acetate,
cotton, mohair and rayon
with aluminum inlay
weft; 36¾ by 63 inches.

*This weaving is in response to
a conversation concerning the
poverty of artists as opposed to
those who create marketable
items and "laugh all the way
to the bank." Since I probably
would not be making any trips
to the bank, I needed to
establish a different bank in
which to store my wealth. I
decided to bank on the river of
life, and laugh all the way—
from the sheer joy of living
and the pleasure of weaving it!*

B

David H. Kaye

LINEN
Linen; 44 by 59½ inches.

C

Kari Ann Arnold

MOODS I
Cotton; painted warp,
twill weaves; 34 by 52
inches.

D

Alice Pickett

UNTITLED
Cotton and linen double
weave with a painted
warp; 4 by 5 feet.

A

B
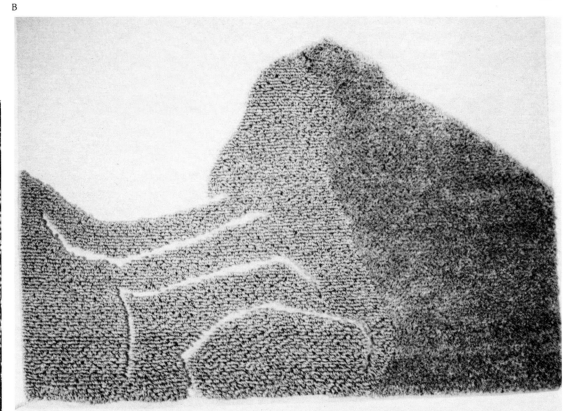

A

C

D

E
Judy Branfman
A THOUSAND VOICES
Handwoven warp bro-
cade tapestry, warp ikat,
warp painting and weft
brocade using hand dyed
linen, wool, cotton, cloth,
plastic, sea grass,
chenilles, mixed fibers
and jute; 33 by 35 inches.
*This piece reflects my growing
concern with the woven
surface, and excitement with
using materials that may seem
to be in contrast with each
other, to create that
surface . . .*

F
Chris Ledoux Hall
IMPRESSION SUNRISE
Cotton, rayon, syn-
thetics; ikat warp and
inlayed weft; 18½ by 35
inches.

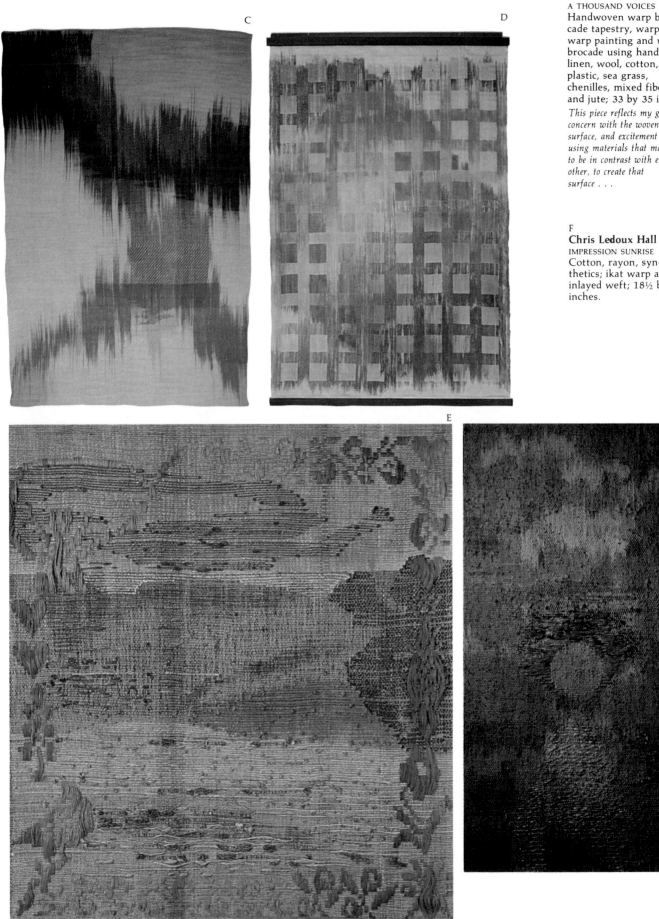

E

F

Jeff Glenn

TRANSFORMATION

Warp faced and weft faced tapestry of linen, rayon, flax, sisal, coconut husk, tree roots and cotton; 6 by 3 feet.

B

Patricia Fox

MEXICAN TAPESTRY

Tapestry and warp faced weave with cotton twine, and printed images; 18 by 24 inches.

This is one of a four-part series. Each tapestry has more and more of the image filled in.

C

Peg McNair

LIMNED SILK

Tapestry with soumak and twining using natural silk, wool and linen; 36 by 52 inches.

D

Roni Zimmer

SYMPHONIC IMPROVISATION
IN TWO MOVEMENTS

Cotton satin weave with painted warp and silk embroidery; 40 by 48 by 3 inches.

B

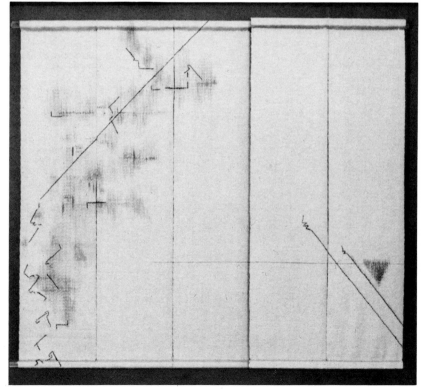

A

C

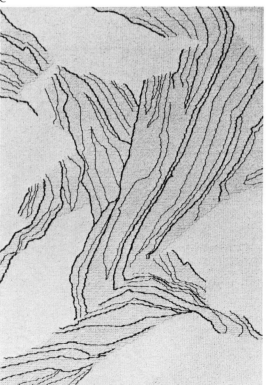

D

E
Nancy Belfer
GARDEN FRAGMENT
Woven viscose rayon
with direct-dye applica-
tion to warp; 72 by 38
inches. Photo by Stephen
Mangione.

F
Mollie H. Fletcher
WEATHER
Wool and cotton; tabby
ground with hand picked
brocade; 16 by 14½
inches.
*During the last two years, my
work has come to be influenced
by the study of ancient textiles.
I feel a commitment to making
fine textiles which have an
appreciation of time, detail,
and personal record—so much
a part of historic textiles.
Therefore, I use hand dyed,
natural fibers to express my
own, very personal imagery.*

G
Cynthia H. Neely
KINETIC STRUCTURES
Linen, cotton; double
weave with pick-up; 29
by 95 inches.

E

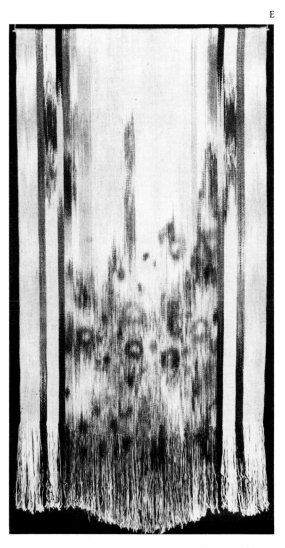

F

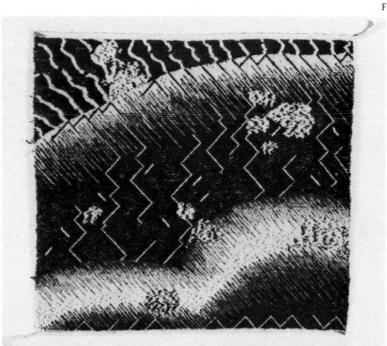

G

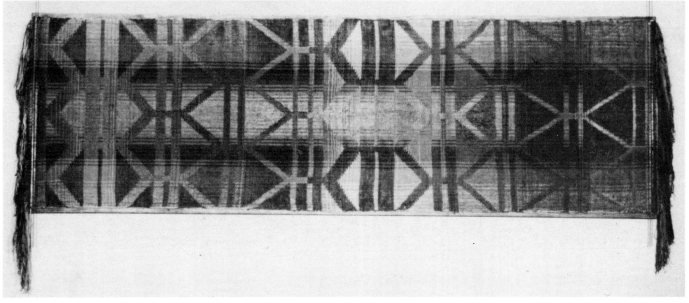

19

A
Linda James
MARK SERIES I
Cotton, double ikat; 33
by 49 inches.
The MARK SERIES *was
inspired by the paintings of
Mark Rothko. My intention
was to try to achieve with dyed
fiber the sensuality and
spirituality of color that
Rothko achieved in his
paintings. I share his belief
that color is a vehicle for basic
human emotions.*

B
Sarah G. Vincent
BEYOND THE BLUE
Plain woven, double ikat
with noil silks and acid
dyes; 52 by 60 inches.

C
Zorine Rinaldi
BINSWANGER
Woven inlay with cotton,
linen, synthetics and
monofilament, painted
with acrylic polymers; 31
by 69 inches.

A

B

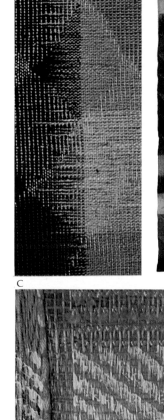

B

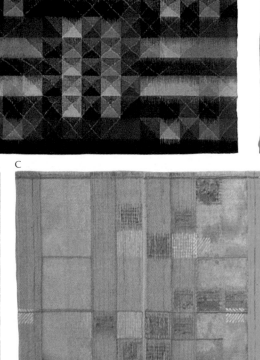

C

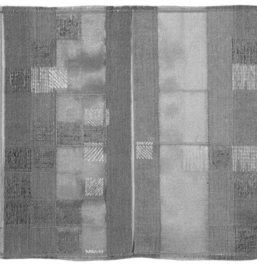

C

D

Sara L. Baker
IN MEMORY OF THE ADOBE
Woven wool, cotton and
synthetics, painted with
acrylics; 72 by 48 inches.

E

Barbara Jurgensen
REFLECTING ON A TIME
Linen, cotton, rayon, silk,
mylar, cotton cording,
wool; double weave and
plain weave; 35½ by 85
by 2 inches.

F

Jana Vander Lee
LONE STAR STATEMENT
Linen and polyester
warp; linen and rayon
weft, with sewing thread
inlay; 17 by 18 inches.

*This is a salute to the Lone
Star State, affirming my
statement as a Texas weaver.
It grew from a response to an
art critic's review of one of my
shows which was labeled
"craft" because the art was
done in fiber.
As a matter of fact
material is immaterial.
What matters is form
transforming form
spanning the space of time.*

G

Maria Ciechomski
LEAF
Wool, acrylic; 86 by 58
inches.

D

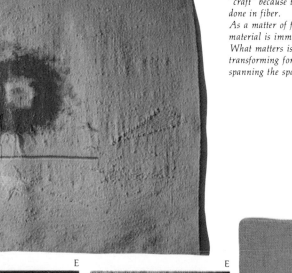

E

F

E

G

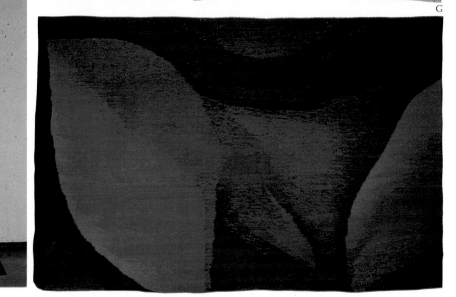

21

A

Myra Bohannon Serrins
FALL IMPRINT
Wool on linen tapestry,
soumak and Swedish
rosepath pattern; 68 by
57 inches.

*I see my tapestries as
drawings, and the patterning
allows me to play with the
surface—impress images into
it, or build up the surface. I'm
aiming at an embossed effect.*

B

Gail Van Slyke
FRONTRANGE COLORADO
Warp faced plain weave
of rayon fiber; cut and
stitched; 8 by 4 feet.

*Inspired by the uplifting,
tilting and folding geologic
formations along the
frontrange foothills of the
Colorado Rockies.*

A

A

B

B

C

Dana Romeis
DESCENT I
Trapunto and channel
quilting on commercially
woven brushed denim;
each panel 16 by 16
inches.

D

Patti Mitchem
LIGHT REVEALED
Perle cotton; warp rep
weave; 28 by 44 inches.

*Using subtle shading of colors
in conjunction with the warp
rep weave, I can give the
appearance of light shining
through.*

C

D   D

A
Henry Easterwood
RED GARDEN II
Tapestry, wool on linen;
74 by 96 inches.
*My designs are derived from
imaginary landscape forms,
and are a combination of my
strong interests in color and
contrasting textures.*

C
Sheila O'Hara
AXEL OF INCIDENCE
Wool and rayon twill
with triple warp; 72 by
36 inches.

B
Judith Poxson Fawkes
SEPTEMBER PRECIPITATION
Linen double weave; 40
by 55 inches.

A

B

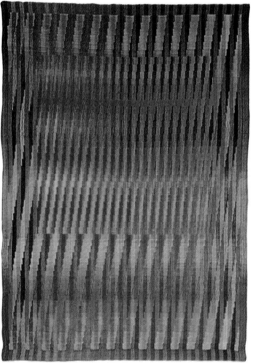

C

C

24

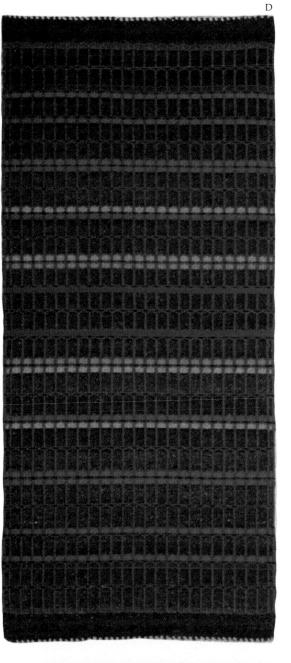

D

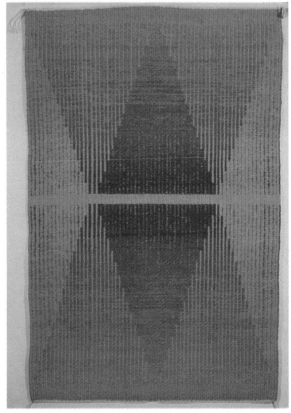

E

F

Laurel M. Moranz
RUG
Three-harness krokbragd
with handspun wool and
linen; 2 by 4 feet.
*I want to create objects that
are functional as well as
pleasing in design. A rug in
an environment is seen on a
daily basis and should
contribute in a positive way in
its effect on life itself.*

E
Elizabeth Caspari
SUNBURST
Flat woven rug of linen
and wool; 47 by 76
inches.

F
Karen Chapnick
EFFUSIONS
Interlocking braids of
hand dyed sisal; 96 by 45
inches.

A

Barbara Heller
STONEWALL SERIES TWO:
AFRICA
Wool on cotton; 3 by 3¾
feet.

Walls are superb metaphors:
Do they keep out or keep in?

B

Beatrice Moore
OTRO MUNDO
Handspun, naturally dyed
wool and mohair, glass
beads and leather; 48 by
84 inches.

This piece was woven on a
Navajo loom and the beadwork
applied onto the leather to
make shapes of tetrahedrons
(floating shades on blue and
black).

C

Susan D. Summa
MAJOR WAYNE'S FOLLY
Loom knitted wool strips
assembled on cotton
canvas; 90 by 90 inches.

This tapestry was inspired by
the story of a Texan (Major
Wayne), who arranged for the
importation of camels (with
two Egyptian handlers) for use
by the Texas Cavalry. The
camels came to an ill-fated end
when they and the Egyptian
handlers were captured during
the Civil War.

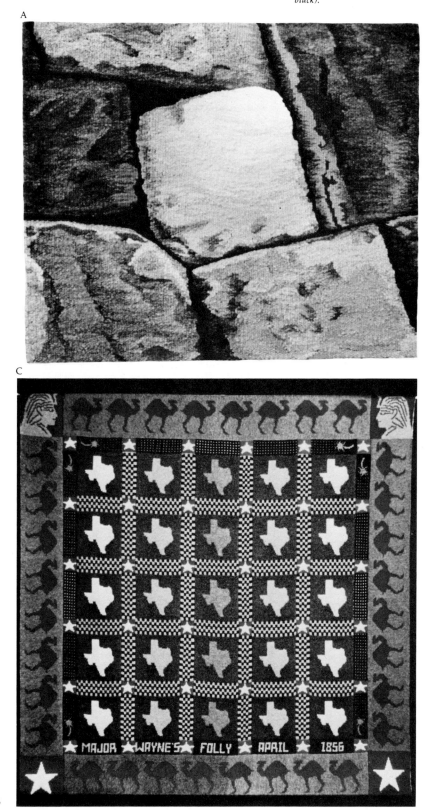

D

Elinor Steele
VARIATIONS ON A THEME
Wool and cotton on
cotton warp tapestry; 77
by 50 inches.

*I use a mathematical approach
to design by combining
geometric shapes of colors that
are numerically mixed to
produce a simple statement
which will express balance and
strength.*

E

Sally Barker
PLANT TAPESTRY
Double interlocked
tapestry of linen, rayon
and cotton; 6 by 5 feet.

D

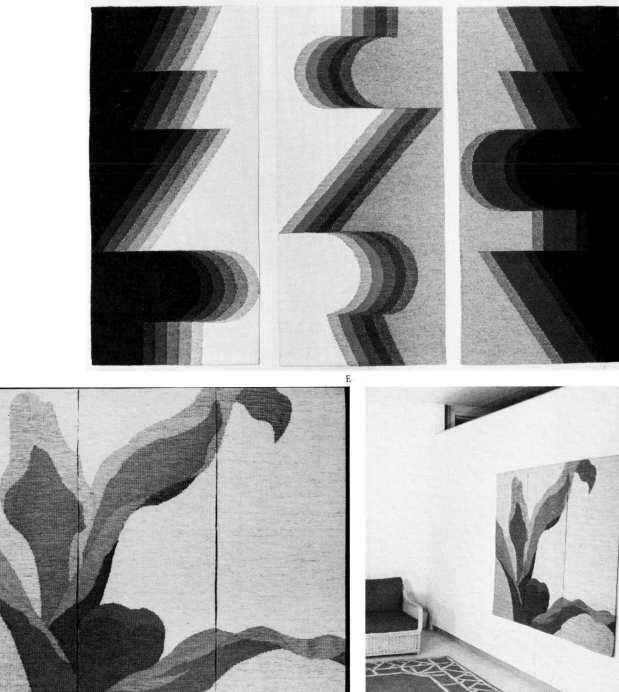

E

E

A

Lindy Andersen Brigham
PERSIAN RUG IN IKAT
Ikat weft on wool, linen
warp; Cushing dyes; 4 by
6 feet.

B

Zofia Dlugopolska
THUNDERSTORM
Wool on cotton tapestry;
58 by 73 inches.

C

Nancy Berry
UNTITLED
Cotton tapestry with
painted warp, using
Water Tex textile paint;
24 by 50 inches.

D

Kristin Carlsen Rowley
MUTATIONS
Naturally dyed wool
tapestry rug; 45 by 84
inches.
*I design directly on the loom,
drawing on motifs I've seen in
Oriental rugs and folk
designs. One can note changes
in my perception of the rug as
it progressed from bottom to
top.*

A

B

C

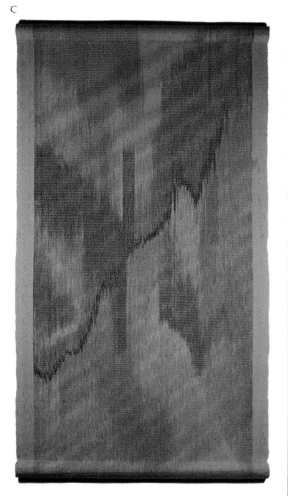

D

E

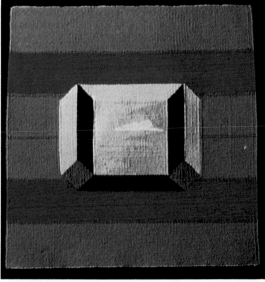

F

H

E
Sally Bachman
RHYTHM OF MOUNTAINS I
Hand dyed wool and linen tapestry; 32 by 30 inches.

Color is a challenge, and I am constantly striving to obtain new horizons in the relationship of hues as they exist among the New Mexico mountains, sky and vegetation. Precision is a dominant factor in my dyeing. I conceive a color scheme in a purely emotional manner, and proceed to dye the hues in a highly controlled method of color blending.

F
Elyse Coulson
WINDOW DREAM
Navajo and tapestry technique with Berga and Lopi wool; 24 by 24 inches.

G
Lucy Ann Warner
IN THE SILENCE OF TIME, ONLY THE HEARTBEAT OF ROCKS
Woven wool, rayon, linen and silk with CIBA dyes; 80 by 47 inches.
This tapestry is mounted on cloth-covered plywood and hung several inches out from the wall so that it "floats".

H
Momo Nagano
AKAGAWA
Linen, wool, reindeer hair; 6 by 8 feet.
Akagawa is the Japanese word for "red river."

I
Diane Itter
TAPIS 3
Hand dyed wool weft on linen warp; weft face tapestry woven in strips and later attached; 10 by 7 feet.

G

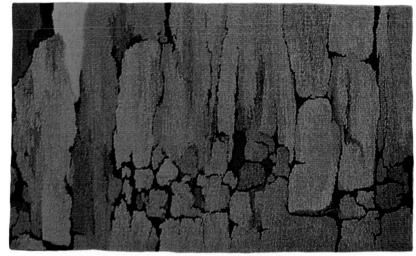

I

29

A
Deborah Corsini
HOUR GLASS
Linen, wool; naturally
dyed yarns (some
handspun yarns); 96 by
45 inches.

*Time and timeless concepts are
important elements of this
work, because of the nature of
tapestry, the slow building of
line upon line of weaving, and
the eternal quality of weaving
tapestries.*

B
Claudia Fraser Stieber
HANGING JAPANESE LANTERN
Woven linen and wool;
acid etching on glass; 19
by 19 inches.

A

B

C
Linda Brookshire
UNTITLED
Wool tapestry; 24 by 30
inches.

D
Mollie H. Fletcher
GRID
Wool, linen and silk;
tabby ground with hand
picked brocade; 34½ by
18 inches.

C   D

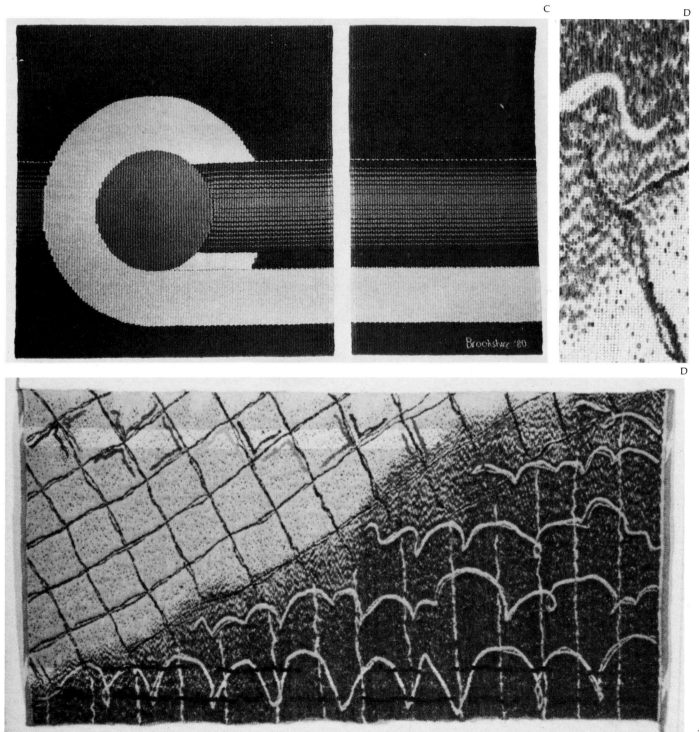

D

Linda Brookshire
UNTITLED
Wool tapestry; 24 by 30
inches.

A
Lillian Elliott
LINE TAPESTRY
Wool on cotton; 4 by 6
feet.

D
Cynthia Schira
PRAIRIE GRASS
Cotton, rayon and linen
plain weave with
supplementary wefts; 64
by 50 inches.

B
Wendy R. Weiss
UNTITLED
Linen and cotton with
warp ikat and inter-
locking weft; 66 by 45
inches.

C
Carolyn Mason Ferrell
TRANSFIGURATION
Double woven and dip
dyed wool; 32 by 50
inches.

A

B

B

C

D

E

Tommye McClure
CANTALOUP
Hand dyed wool using
Procion dyes; six-harness
pick-up weave with inlay
weft; 16 by 16 inches.

F

Joyce Marquess
KNOTWORK
Woven wool on linen,
trapunto center; 30 by 40
inches.

E

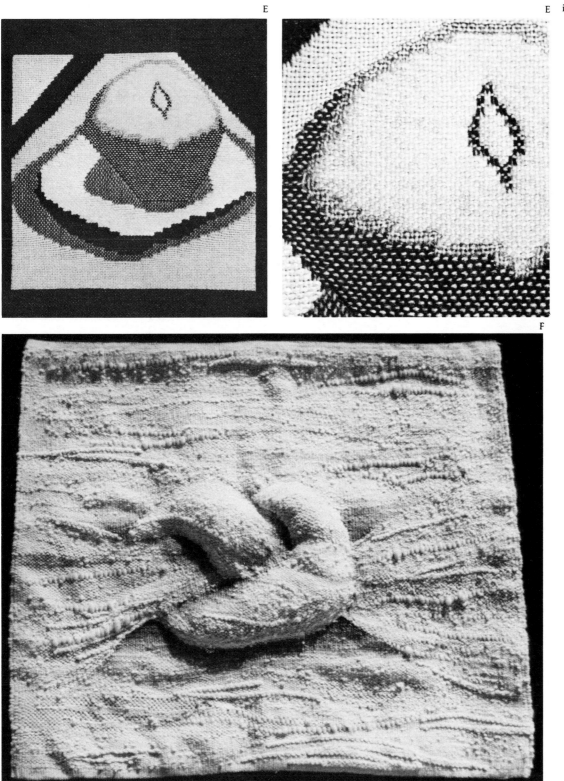

E

F

A

Jean Nordlund
WOODED LANE
Double woven wool; 3 by
4 feet.
*All of my work involves the
bold movement and intersection
of color in double woven form.
I work on a 24-harness loom,
often re-tying treadles in one
piece to allow more design
flexibility. The wool yarns are
chemically dyed as needed to
produce fine gradations of
color.*

B

Bonnie Wiegner
FIREWORKS BY GANDALF
Linen and wool tapestry
with hatching techniques;
18 by 40 inches.

C

**Margaret Portman
Griffey**
UNKNOWN OCEAN
Aubusson tapestry of
linen and wool; 80 by 60
inches.
*The geometric nature of my
work is a logical result of the
grid-like structure and basis of
a woven fabric. The work also
reflects an interest in the
illusion of space, shifting
planes in space and
contradictory indications of
spatial definition.*

D

Mark Adams—*Designer*
**San Francisco Tapestry
Workshop**—*Weavers*
WHITE BLOCK
Wool Aubusson tapestry;
46 by 53 inches. Photo by
Victor Budnik.

E

Cecilia Blomberg
THE STAIRCASE
Traditional tapestry;
wool, linen weft on linen
warp; 43 by 33 inches.
*This tapestry is based on a
black and white photograph by
Tina Modotti, 1923.*

A

B

C

D

E

F

F
Joanne Soroka
WEAVING WITH THE WIND
THE IRISES AND THE REEDS
TAPESTRIES OF GOLD
Linen, wool and chenille
on cotton warp, Gobelin
tapestry; 60 by 95 inches.
*Part of the inspiration for this
tapestry comes from Japanese
screens.*

G
Sarah D. Haskell
GREGSON LANDSCAPE
Tapestry with rosepath
threading of wool,
cotton, metallic and
rayon; 8 by 4 feet.

H
Mark Adams—*Designer*
**San Francisco Tapestry
Workshop**—*Weavers*
HAENA POINT
Wool Aubusson tapestry;
67 by 54¾ inches. Photo
by Victor Budnik.

I
Sally Bowker
DUNN COUNTY LANDSCAPE
Tapestry of handspun
and naturally dyed cotton
and wool; 13 by 19
inches.

G

G

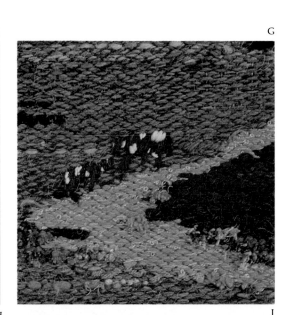

H

I

A

Donna Lee Lish
LAMENTATION CLOAK
Cotton; 30 by 24 by 1
inches.

*This work is composed of
hundreds of individually folded
and discharged strips, which
are sewn together.*

B

Gail Johnson Resen
BREAKING FORTH
Warp faced weaving of
linen with brass rods in
weft; unwoven warp
dropped forward and
wrapped with metallic
thread; 12 by 24 inches.

*By weaving rods into a tight,
warp faced linen fabric, I can
create greater dimension in a
piece which often produces
strong shadows and reflective
effects. A frequent theme
running through my work is
that of building a structure
and then exposing it . . .*

A

A

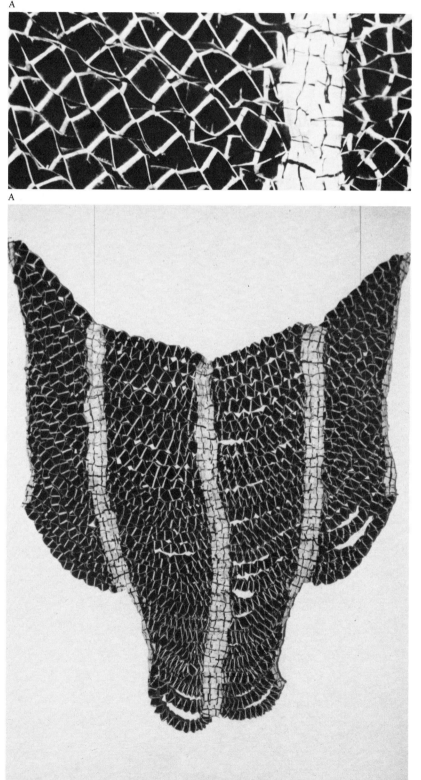

B

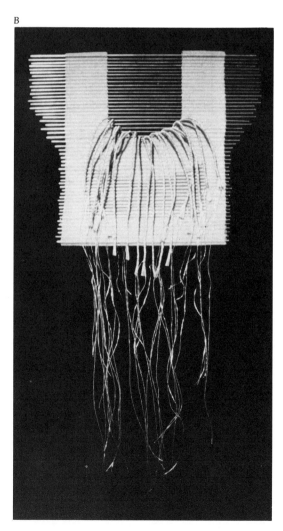

C

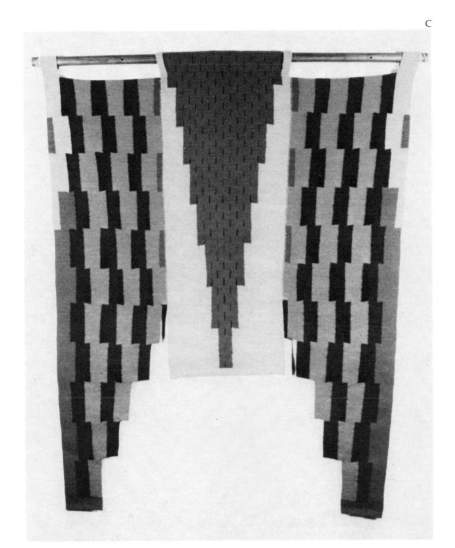

C
Rochelle Newman
TRIPLET
Cotton and wool
interlocked tapestry; 47
by 60 inches.

D
Susan Wilchins
STUDY IN BLACK AND WHITE
Eight-harness double
weave of wool and linen
worked in a weft faced
manner; 36¾ by 23½
inches.

*The structure of this piece, and
others I have done in a similar
manner, provides the
opportunity to work with
optical illusions. I like the
mystery that this structure
conveys.*

D

D

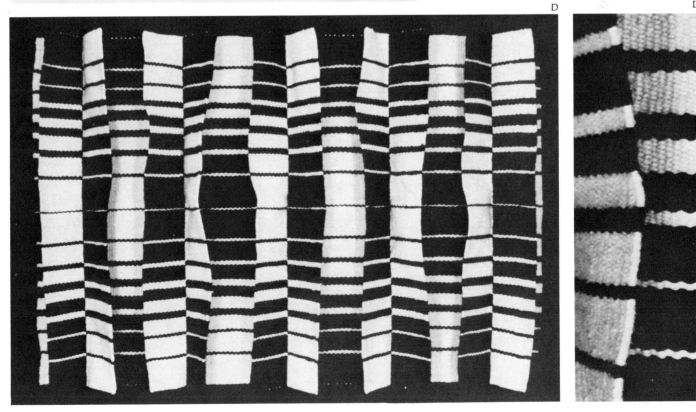

37

A
Ruth Ginsberg-Place
POPPIES #3
Wool, rayon, cloth-strip
tapestry with warp
bleeding; 36 by 28 inches.
Photo by Ken Clark.

B
Helena Hernmarck
POPPIES
Tapestry of linen, wool
and synthetic fibers; 20
by 11 feet.
*What I like about the poppy
tapestry is its scale and
simplicity. The bright yellow
seen against the deep dark blue
is as crisp as the look of the
building in which it hangs,
One Dallas Centre. The
challenge in weaving this
tapestry was to achieve the
transparency of the fragile
petals and the delicate green of
the out-of-focus grass, which
contrasts nicely with the
clarity of the flowers. The
weaving technique used is a*
*continuous tabby weft with two
supplementary wefts. Areas of
precision are handpicked and
areas that are blurred and out
of focus are sometimes done in
a rosepath pattern. These
supplementary weft rows are
woven with a thick bundle of
yarn, up to 12 threads. There
are up to 50 different color-
combinations of bundles in one
row across the width.*

A

B

B

C

C

E

Martha Matthews
PEARS
Wool, linen, cotton,
polyester on cotton warp;
49 by 39 inches.
*I made the cartoon from a
photo I had taken and wove
the tapestry on a high warp
loom with the cartoon behind
the warp.*

D
Yael Lurie—*Designer*
Jean Pierre Larochette—
Weaver
LIGHT FLOWER
Aubusson tapestry of
wool and silk; 47 by 53
inches. Photo by Victor
Budnik.

E
Nancy Austen
EGRETS IN A JUNGLE RIVER
Wool and mohair
tapestry; 60 by 56 inches.
*This piece was woven during a
difficult Michigan winter!*

F
Mark Adams—*Designer*
**San Francisco Tapestry
Workshop**—*Weavers*
WHITE PETUNIAS
Wool Aubusson tapestry;
41 by 52 inches. Photo by
Victor Budnik.

D

F

A

Garry St. John Benson

TIP OF YOUR TONGUE

High warp tapestry of
linen and wool; 9½ by 3½
feet.

B

Judi Keen

ASPARAGUS

Wool on cotton tapestry
(Aubusson technique); 36
by 45 inches.

*I work with architects and
interior designers, doing
custom pieces for residential
and commercial interiors, on a
commission basis. I find the
collaborative effort both
challenging and rewarding—
each client and environment
presents an entirely new set of
givens and constantly forces me
in new directions.*

C

Lynn Murray

UNTITLED

Wool and cotton chenille
tapestry; 5 by 7 feet.

*This piece was designed to fit a
stairway wall which rises at
an angle.*

A

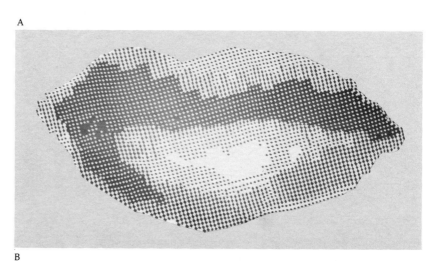

B

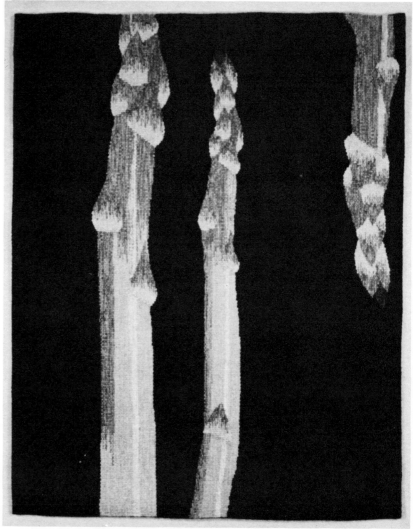

C

D

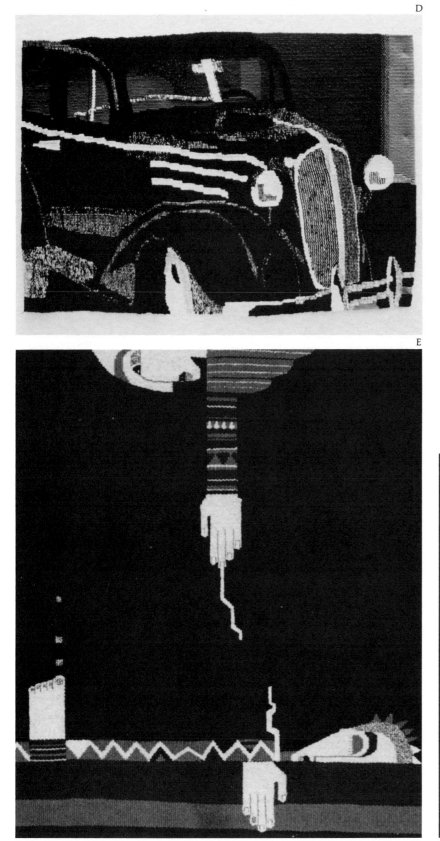

Dean Johns
DAD'S CLASSIC
High warp tapestry of handspun wool with plain weave; 5 by 3 feet.
I use fiber to accentuate my designs, rather than selecting the fiber and building the design from it. Most designs are personal in nature—self-portraits, my children and "family things".

E

Gail Bent
SLEEPING GYPSY
Gobelin tapestry weave of cotton, wool and metallic thread; 42 by 54 inches.

F

Barbara A. Chappell
RAINY DAY VIEW
Linen, wool; 24 by 32 inches.
This tapestry is one of a series that I have been working on, interpreting black and white photographs into pictorial tapestry. It comes from a photograph I took and is woven in black and five shades of grey.

A
Kay J. Denton
RIDE, RIDE, RIDE
Handwoven tapestry of sisal, wool and cotton yarns and rags; 3 by 4 feet.

This handwoven, primitive scene is a memory of a special family visit to an amusement park.

B
Carol A. Mecagni
MOSES IN THE BULRUSHES
Wool, goathair; 24 by 38 inches.

I believe art can tell a story of feelings, of ideas or thoughts— a central theme to alter, add to, or dissect so that it becomes your own.

C
Susan Kelly
BEDECKED
Gobelin tapestry of wool and cotton with 20% of materials hand dyed; 76 by 87 inches.

I want my tapestries to illustrate an image that alternates from abstraction to realism, depending on the focal point or perception of the viewer. I aim for mystery, deception and whimsy. I like to give people an opportunity to think about what they are seeing, and to have a chuckle. For me, art doesn't always have to be a serious statement on life conditions!

D
Kay J. Denton
AND A TREE THAT TOUCHED THE CEILING
Hand hooked wool rag tapestry with burlap foundation; 35½ by 41 inches.

Each of my tapestries are filled with family-owned rag remnants, and often, the checks, tweeds, plaids and blue jean scraps from my children's outgrown clothes add special meaning to each scene. Because the places, people, and events celebrated are real, my rag pictorials become a visual diary for me.

E
Jaroslava Lialia Kuchma
PARROT PIECE
Tabby woven wool, rayon and acrylic; 6 by 4 feet.

A

B

C

D

E

F
David R. Mooney
DISSOLUTION OF THE
I FACULTY
Wool and linen in a
modified Coptic tech-
nique; 47 by 30 inches.
Photo by David R.
Mooney.

G
Cecilia Blomberg
THE SISTERS
Traditional tapestry and
soumak; wool, silver
thread, linen weft on
linen warp; 43 by 42
inches.

*By depicting interactions—
social and environmental—in
the world around us, I am
attempting to reverse the trend
toward technique over content
in fiber art.*

H
Jaroslava Lialia Kuchma
TARTS
Woven rayon, wool,
acrylic and metallic yarn;
82½ by 48 inches.

*Inspiration and ideas are
always around me, and I try
to isolate one which excites me
and develop it through fiber.
The influence, in this case
German expressionistic
painting, served to generate a
process in which I used not
only the medium of fiber, but
also my involvement in
photography, and the support
of close friends who posed for
the idea.*

I
Laurie Gano
TOUCAN
Wool Mexican tapestry
and linear soumak;
acrylic (space dyed); 37
by 32 inches.

F

G

H

I

43

A

Roslyn Logsdon
STUDY IN BROWNS
Rug hooking technique, pulling strips of material through a burlap backing; 28 by 40 inches.

So many things in life are passed by—we forget. Old photographs always bring this to my mind, and STUDY IN BROWNS *is taken from an old tintype that I found, rummaging through old photographs. I felt very close to these two men, even though I never knew them, and I wanted to bring them back—I didn't want them to be forgotten.*

B

Jane Lowell-LaRoque
ME AGAIN
Wool on linen, crackle weave; 14½ by 27½ inches.

C

Elizabeth Nettleton
NOTHING STOPS
Wool and cotton tapestry; 72 by 48 inches.

A

B

C

D

E

F

D
Laurie Gano
PIG IN GRASS
Wool Mexican tapestry
and linear soumak; 37 by
36 inches.

*I learned to weave in Mexico,
and continue to apply the
Mexican tapestry technique to
designs that interest me—
birds, animals and landscape.
I am interested in color and
subtle texture, the creation of
depth, space and patterns in
nature.*

E
**Boithuso (Self-help)
Weavers of Lesotho**
UNTITLED
Tapestry of mohair and
wool; 27 by 43 inches.

F
Jennifer Bennett
THE GREAT SILKIE
Woven tapestry, cotton
warp, wool weft; 19 by
30 inches.

*The Great Silkie is a mythical
seal of Scotland, who comes
ashore as a man to mate with
a woman. Later, he returns to
land to collect his baby and
goes back to the sea to raise the
child as a seal.*

A

Pamela Topham

OFF SHORE FLORIDA: NORTH OF BOYTON INLET

Tapestry of wool, silk and linen; 26 by 38 inches.

This is one of a series of "off-shore" tapestries which started from colored pencil sketches which I did while sailing . . . the sketches just seemed to develop into tapestries!

B

Sherry Owens

ARABESQUE AT TWILIGHT

Hand dyed wool and linen, slit tapestry; 60 by 40 inches.

I am increasingly aware of the world in color, and continue to explore the depth of color. I dye many of the fibers I use to gain more control over the colors. Sometimes the unexpected hues result in new dimensions for future tapestries.

C

Jane Truitt

MAGIC MOUNTAIN

Tapestry of wool rug yarn; 32 by 44 inches.

D

Mark Adams—*Designer* **San Francisco Tapestry Workshop**—*Weavers*

SUNSET WITH PALMS

Wool Aubusson tapestry; 72 by 64¾ inches. Photo by Victor Budnik.

E

Susan Zabawa

FAMILY BEACH SCENE

Cotton tapestry; 22 by 19 inches.

The inspiration for this piece came from the combination of a love for old pictorial tapestries and an old family photograph.

A

B

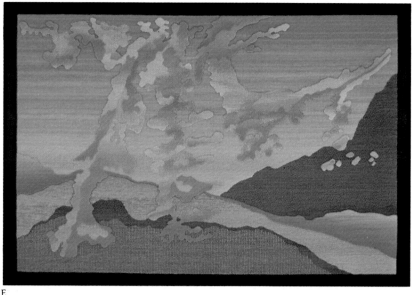

C

D

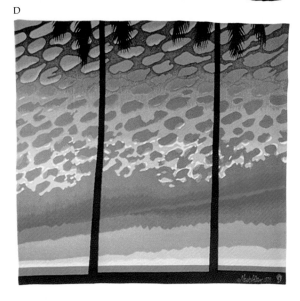

E

THREE
DIMENSIONS

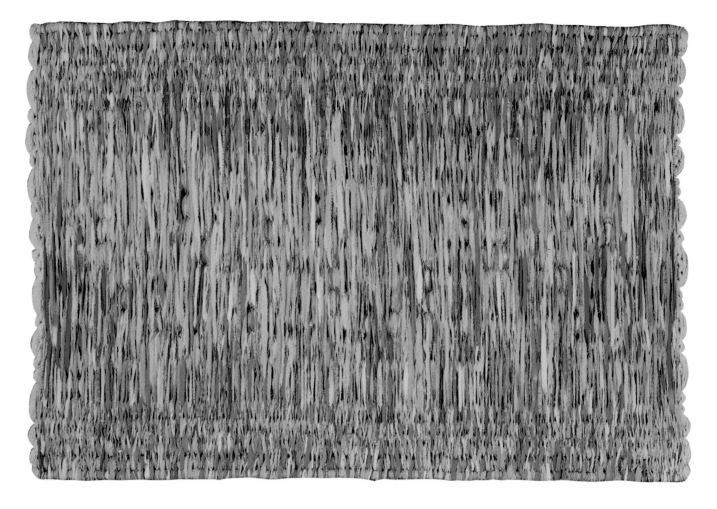

overleaf

Ruth Bright Mordy

EARTHLIFE

Cardwoven cotton, silk, rayon and linen with tie-dye and warp weighting; 108 by 72 by 2½ inches.

Exploring the intricacies of cardweaving encouraged me to expand this technique from its traditional constraints of size and material. To produce my work, I have used common materials including mop string, upholstery trims and the interior fibers of an old rope, as well as silk, cotton, linen and wool. I have also explored the use of systematically tie-dyed fabrics, ripped into warp elements and re-combined into a complex visual surface via cardweaving.

A

Susan Warner Keene

RUMORS OF ATLANTIS

Dyed, buckled tapestry of sisal, cotton and linen; 78 by 78 by 12 inches. Photo by Peter Newman.

B

Ruth Geneslaw

INTERLOCK

Knit tubing of wool, handstitched to stretched muslin; 72 by 36 inches.

C

Becky Clark

PINESTRA

Dyed jute welt cord, wrapped and knotted; 95 by 46 by 6 inches.

A

B
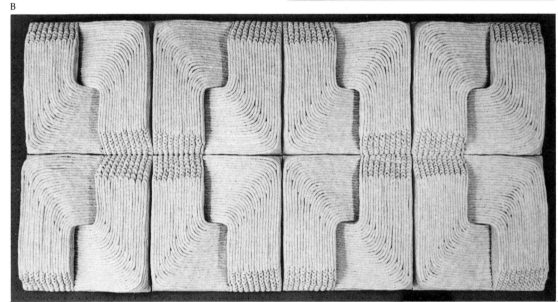

C
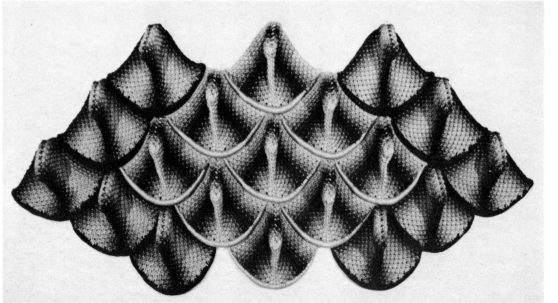

C

D

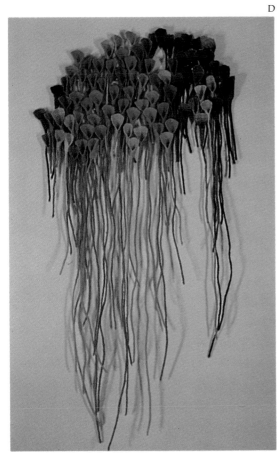

Margaret Getty
IMPRESSION I
Hand dyed wool and linen; double woven tubes, wrapped warp ends; 21 by 43 inches.
My work reflects my own growth and opening as a person which has occurred in the past two years. It has evolved from tightly wrapped warp constructions, to closed tubes and then tubes opening with slits, or opening completely at one end.

E

Sherri Smith
ATHENA
Cotton webbing, worked by hand; 11 by 8 by ¾ feet.

F

Nola Jones
PURPLE VERTICAL
Off-loom weaving of sisal and jute; 44 by 84 by 8 inches.

G

Julie Wallace Keller
THE FALL OF HYMEN'S RULE
Woven gauze and cotton string; 12 by 16 by 4 inches each. Photo by John S. Graves.

H

Ruth Gowell
BRAIDED STUDY II
Warp faced rayon weaving with Procion dyes; 40 by 30 by 4 inches.

E

F

G

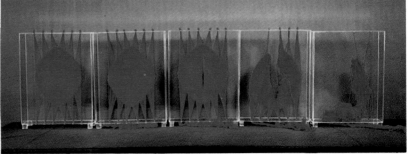

H

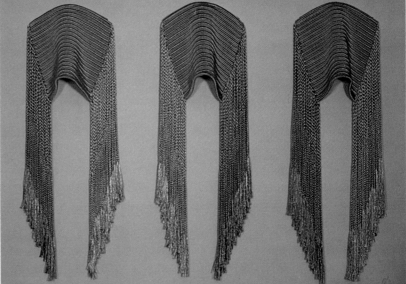

A
Sigrid Meier
KNOTS
Wool, linen, silk, cotton,
synthetics; 6 by 12 feet.

*My approach to weaving is
a sculptural one, and I like
my work to have a
subdued elegance.*

B
Pierre Vallauri
TENSION-LIGATURE
Jute canvas and jute,
wrapped and stretched
on frame; 17½ by 26
inches.

*My work is a personal form of
meditation.*

C
Laurie Gross
CONGREGATION OF 22
Woven linen; 20 by 18 by
1 inches.

*This is part of a body of work
based on the Jewish prayer
shawl, the tallis. I am
working within the guidelines
of religious tradition and
adding my personal
commentary.*

A

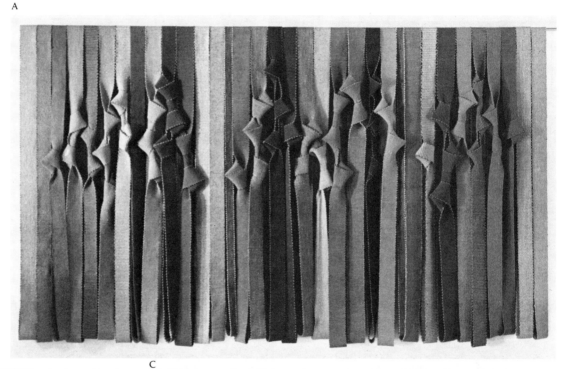

B

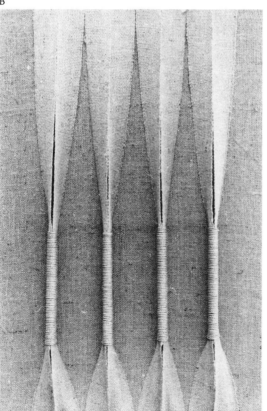

C

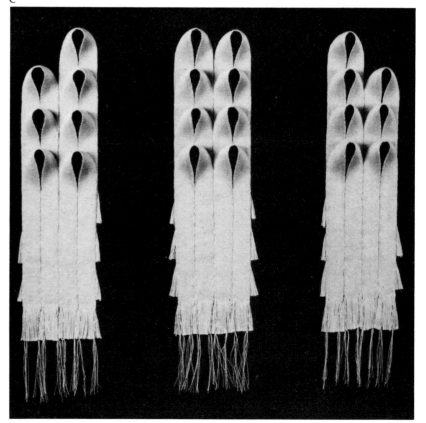

50

D

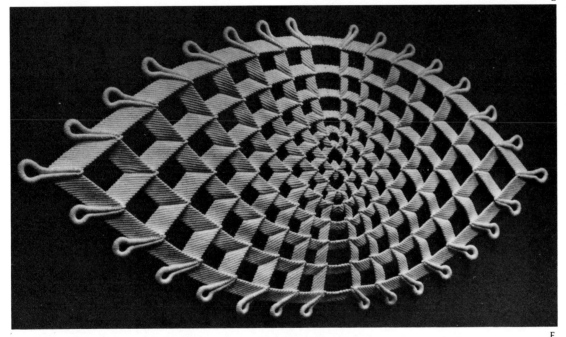

D

Angela Kosta Driessen
SECRET COMPARTMENTS
Latex paint on cotton
fabric which is sized and
formed before painting;
56 by 50 by 3½ inches.

E

Joan Michaels-Paque
CATENARY CURVES
Knotted, wrapped and
woven synthetic fiber;
117 by 71 by 5 inches.
Photo by Henry P.
Paque.

*I am a sculptor, and construct
and create architectural
structures based on my
experiments with topology
(study of warped surfaces). I
am concerned with concepts
and ideas, and use whatever
flexible, linear material that
best expresses these ideas.*

F

Joyce Campbell
FLAMINGO
Hand dyed sisal and
wool; 5 by 4½ feet.

E

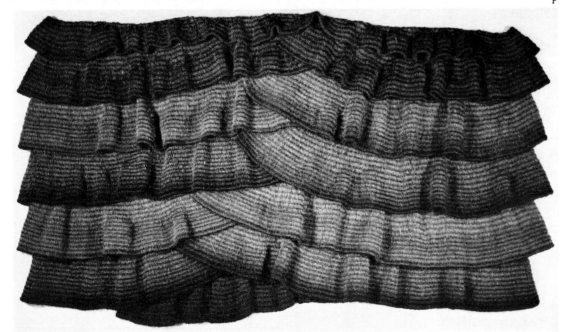

F

A
Tetsuo Kusama
WALL-D
Double woven cotton; 74 by 24 by 2 inches.

B
Susan Iverson
CALM CONVERSATION
Wool on linen warp tapestry; 66 by 66 inches.

C
Ann Savageau
FOURTEEN SQUARED
Cotton webbing on a handwoven background; colored with textile paint; 19 by 36 inches.

During the past three years one of my concerns has been to explore the grid as a basic structural element—it is, after all, the primary structure of weaving. The background of this piece is a plain-weave. Each row of the foreground consists of one long strip of webbing which is pulled through the background, folded, pulled through the background again, and so on.

D
Lesley E. Shearer
WAVES
Experimental multi-harness weave with hand dyed wool; 6 by 3 feet.

E
Paul O'Connor
MOBILE COLONNADE
Cotton and polyester double weave with wood inserts; 15 by 4 to 9 by 1 inches.

I feel it is important to mount double woven fabric so that it can be viewed from different angles.

A
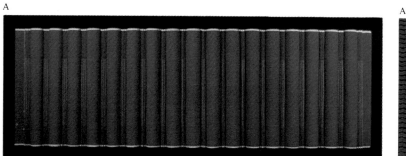

A

B
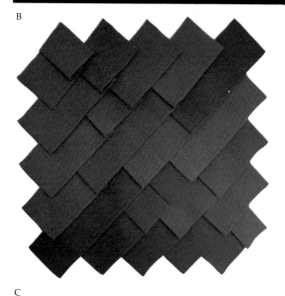

C
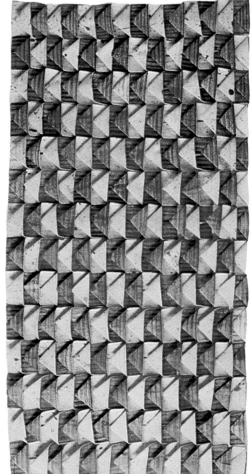

C

D

D
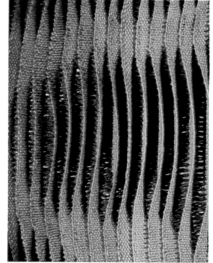

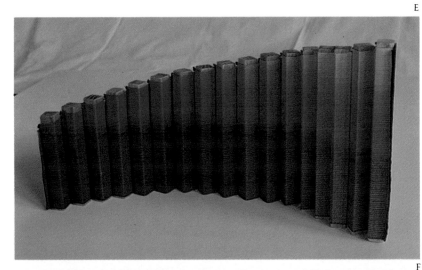

E

F
Jean Singerman Weiss
PLANE INTERSECT: DELTA
Tubular double weave of
wool, sisal, cotton, coir
and jute; post-weaving
construction; 96 by 60 by
6 inches.

G
Michi Ouchi
OVERLAPPED COLOR AND
SHADOW—PINK GREY
Wool, cotton; hand dyed;
double weave, tapestry;
24 by 23 inches.
*My main concern is color and
interaction of color, light and
shadow. Richness in
simplicity. I try to obtain this
by using simple geometric
patterns and a few hues of
color.*

H
Judith Page
LANDSCAPE WITH CON-
CEALED MONUMENTS
Photo collage on cotton
and nylon, using Xerox
transfer, cut into strips
and woven; 6½ by 6½
feet.
*I am intrigued by the idea of
undiscovered monuments
hidden beneath oceans, sands,
grass and jungle—formerly
vast and powerful cities have
melted into the landscape.*

I
Joan Seifert
DESERT
Wool plain weave with
pulled warp; metallic
added to surface; 30 by
26 inches.

F

G

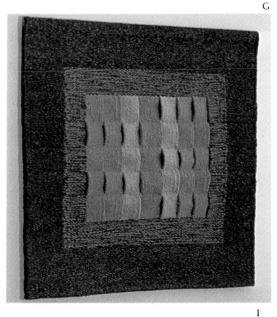

H

H

I

A
Chris Craig
INFO-PACS
Handmade paper; 24 by 18 inches.

B
Peg Andersen
RAIN GUTTERS
Warp faced ikat with Procion dyed wool; each panel 9 by 21 inches.

C
Joan Vendley
VERNAL EQUINOX
Manipulated warp weaving of linen and wool; 32 by 44 by 5 inches.

D
Joan Russell
WHITE CIRCLE ON ROPES
Handwoven strips and handmade rope of wool, cotton, linen and rayon; 8 by 8 feet.

E
Misako Tanaka
UNTITLED
Linen and cotton cloth;
12 by 12 by 118 inches.

F
David H. Kaye
UNTITLED #5
Plain weave and twill of
sisal; 48½ by 66½ by 20
inches.
*The development of my textile
work has been methodical and
careful. I hope to create work
that has strength, integrity
and a vital spirit.*

G
Jacqueline Boggs
UNTITLED
Knitted, interwoven
acrylic yarn; 44 by 50
inches.
*Knitting is a beautifully
simple technique which readily
develops out of its own nature,
stretching and curling, to form
a wide variety of basic, two-
dimensional structures.*

H
Christine Nobles Heller
FACETS STUDY #1
Woven satin fabric and
cotton warp; 15 by 15 by
2 inches.

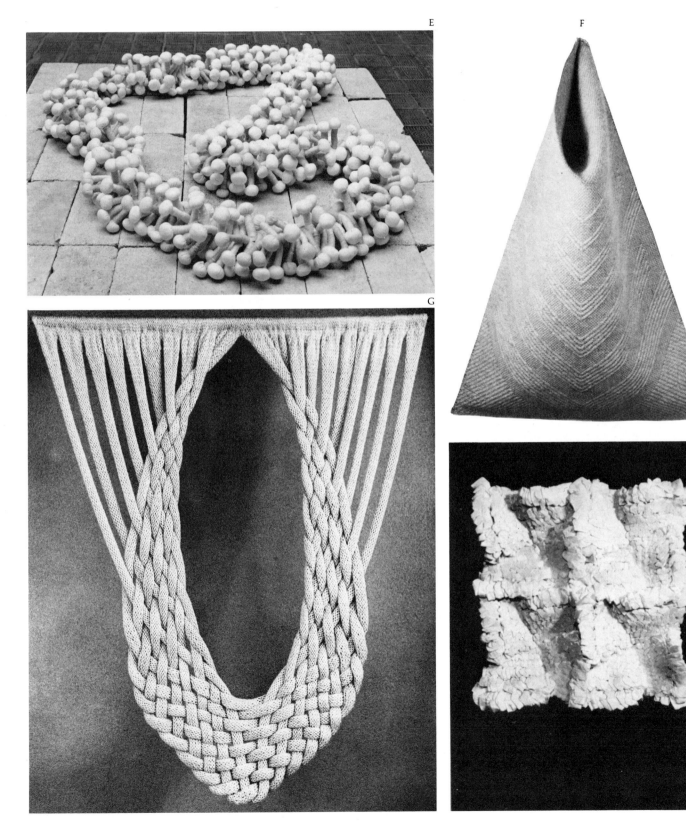

E

F

G

H

A
April May
TULIPS
Cotton, wool, linen,
mohair; Theo Moorman
technique; 2 panels—48
by 80 inches each.

B
Linda Nelson Bryan
BACKWATERS
Silk painting, using gutta
resist and French silk
dyes; 5 banners, 4 by 22
feet each.

C
Laura Militzer
ON WINGS OF DREAMS
Dip dyed silk on wood; 4
by 4 by 7 feet.
*I am exploring the movement
of color in space.*

B

A

C

C

D

E

56

F

D
Libby Platus
AFTERNOON ROMANCE
Maxi-cord on a sisal core; cross-tension knotting; 10 by 12 by 2 feet.

E
Dot Replinger
WHITE HORSE INN
Double woven wool; 4 by 5 feet to 5 by 15 feet.

This piece was commissioned by a restaurant owner who wanted some separation between the two levels of the dining area. He gave me complete freedom in design and color choice . . . a super client!

F
Clara Karlan
Vivian Fikus
Mickey Samara
UNTITLED
Macrame, wrapping, coiling and sculptural knotting with bleached jute, bulky acrylic; 18 by 20 feet.

We are a designer, an artist and a crafter, who have combined our talents and efforts to do unusual one-of-a-kind fiber works, often on a commissioned basis.

G
Priscilla Sage
TINCTORIAL SPIRAL
Silver mylar fabric with disperse dyes (dry method); 12 by 4¼ feet.

The fabric is stitched to ½-inch foam rubber and then pleated. Two pieces of steel airplane cable run through the spiral. When the cable is tight, the pleating occurs, and the spiral is created. Air currents keep the sculpture in constant movement.

G

G

H
Cindy Snodgrass
FLOWERS AREN'T FOREVER
Nylon, sewn; 35 by 30 by 35 feet.

H

A
Kriss Jana Olsen
C.O.D.
Plain woven wool with wrapping; 60 by 47 inches.

B
Grafiella Weber-Grassi
SHIFTED DIAGONALS
Tapestry of woven sisal; 29 by 23½ by 2 inches. Photo by Mildred Leipzig.

C
Judi Keen
ORIGAMI I
Cotton; warp faced plain weave; wrapping; 48 by 40 by 4 inches.

D
Dana Romeis
SHADOW RELIEF
Silk, porcelain and pearl cotton on a loom-woven ground; 31 by 31 by 3½ inches.
I wanted to create a floating design element that cast strong shadows on the woven ground.

A

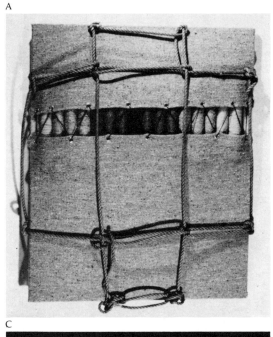

B

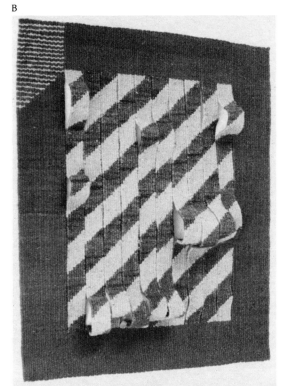

C

D

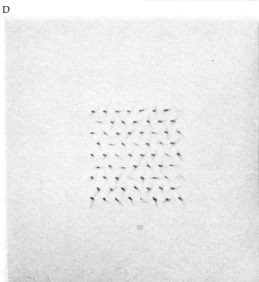

D

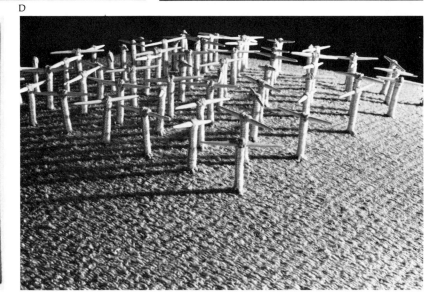

E

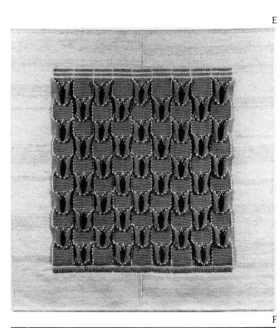

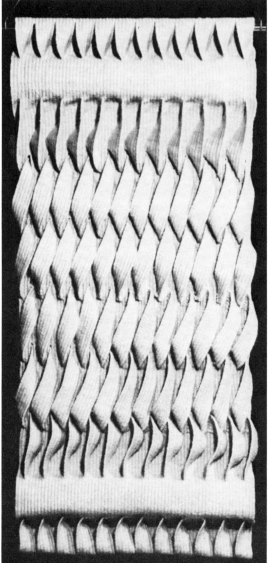
F

G

E
Sigrid Meier
WINDOW
Handwoven warp and weft faced tapestry of wool and linen; 54 by 56 inches. Photo by Bruce A. Blank.

F
Niki Guyer
UNTITLED
Linen, slit tapestry; 3½ by 4 feet.

I work with linen, usually undyed, because my concern is with line and shadow.

G
Susan Venable Nelson
PEKING FENCE
Twill and plain weave of sisal and nylon; 71 by 76 by 11 inches.

I've been working with this fence theme for the past three years, exploring the relationship of fences as barriers—psychological and physical protections and defenses.

A

Katherine Howe

COLOR CARD SERIES: DRAKE
AND HUNTER'S GREEN
Warp face weave with
linen warp, torn canvas
weft; applique and collage
of paper, ribbons with
paint, dye and nail polish;
18 by 18 inches.

B

Fran Cutrell Rutkovsky

ROY G. BIV-PANELS
Cotton, brushed wools,
mohair, synthetic blends;
tapestry strips joined by
wrapping edges; 34 by 32
inches.

C

Marilyn Meltzer

FRAGMENT
Gold cord, silk wrapping;
tapestry; 36 by 22 by 3
inches.

D

Harriet Quick

NOCCA CURTAIN
Knotless netting and
crochet with binder
twine, rug yarn,
computer tape; 3 panels,
60 by 17 feet each.
*In 1979 I worked as an
artist-in-residence at the New
Orleans Center for the
Creative Arts (NOCCA), a
public high school for students
gifted in music, drama,
writing, dance and the visual
arts. With the help of Jan and
Frank Gross, visual arts
instructors, and sixty art
students, this three-panel stage
curtain was constructed, over a
two-month time period. Each
screen was mapped out on the
floor like a jigsaw puzzle—
each student worked on one
small section and then joined it
with the other work.*

A

B

D

C

D

E

Kay Lee Willens

UNTITLED

Double cloth pick-up of wool, painted rayon and clear mylar; 40 to 65 by 67 by 2 inches.

Using a mylar weft eliminated the need for a warp faced weave to show the painted color warp. In addition, it enabled me to achieve a highly reflective and luminescent surface.

F

Francis Wilson

TJURUNGA III

Combination of macrame and personal techniques with coco fiber, colored with acrylic paint; radius—59 inches.

G

Gregory Patrick Garvey

1340-43

White spandex, suspended and stretched by fishing line and lighted with Kliegl 1340-43 ellipsoidals.

I am pursuing a career of lighting, sound and scenic design for theater, television and film. Light, form produced by tension and time (transformation by changes in color) are the components of my work.

G

G

A
Carol L. Baker

SILENCE

Screen printed linen, direct dyed in gradating system of color; ten units installed separately, four inches apart to create an all-over fabric relief; 42 by 43 by 4 inches.

B
Gail Van Slyke

TRIAD

Rayon/mohair blend; honeycomb weave; 54 by 72 by 6 inches.

C
Meri Ann Walsh

PAPERFORM I

Woven, plied, spun and varnished paper; 34 by 40 by 4 inches.

I use a Japanese technique called Boumaki in combination with modern Xerography and textured rag or rice papers. This allows me to work and re-work a very delicate image using color and weaving to emphasize or fracture the image.

A

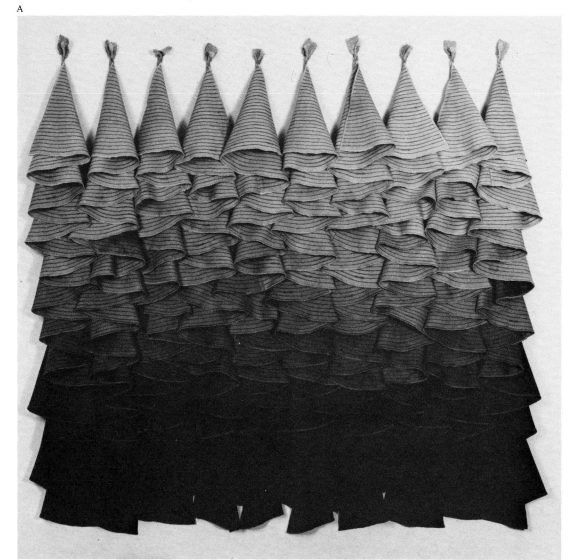

B

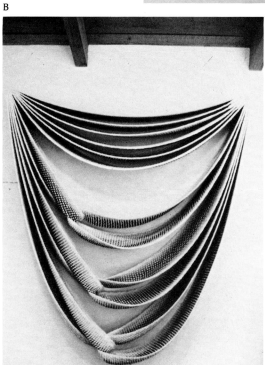

C

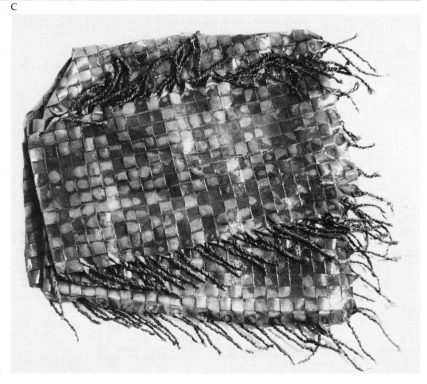

D

Gail Johnson Resen
TOWER I
Linen and wooden
dowels; 11 by 21 by 5
inches.

*A frequent theme running
through my work is that of
building a structure and then
exposing it.*

E

Ralph H. Gates
LOOK MA, NO HANDLE
Broom corn, linen cord;
18 by 34 by 3 inches.

*This is a practical departure
from tradition. The arch was
formed by layering each side
over a small piece of wood and
soaking the broom corn to
shape.*

F

Allan Greedy
CHOICES
Aluminum, bronze;
casting from three-weft
plaited chenille fabric and
batiked paper; 24½ by 19
by 9 inches.

E

F

63

A

Joan Kaufman
TEREBRA
Shaped plain weave of
hand dyed silk; nickel-
plated copper; 6 by 20 by
4 inches.
*The inspiration for this
piece came from a study of
shells and other sea forms.
Metal and silk, two
different and seemingly
incompatible materials are
combined to demonstrate
an essential similarity. The
silk was woven on a floor
loom, molded and set into
the handmade metal form.*

B

Chris Carpenter
NOTHING TO HIDE
Cotton with structural
stitchery; 13 by 19 by 7
inches.

C

Elizabeth Lawrence
WOOZLE COVER
Wool, mohair; 116 by 72
inches.
*This bedcover is double woven,
with the top layer woven
higher than the bottom. The
tension on the top layer
backbeam was loosened and the
layers were beaten down to the
height of the bottom layer. I
believe that artistic and
functional weaving do not have
to be separated—by
combining the two into
something such as a bedcover,
the viewer becomes participant
with the piece.*

D

Marilyn Herrmann
FIRE BASKET
Coiled wool and perle
cotton over fiber-flex
core; 6 by 13 inches.
Photo by Frank
Herrmann.

E

Dennery Kahn
GLASS BASKET SERIES
Slumped Pyrex glass rods
with ceramic underglazes;
12 by 8 by 18 inches.
*Although I use glass, rather
than yarn or fleece, I consider
my baskets as textiles. I
studied glass-making and
weaving at the same time, and
my many years of textile study
influenced my concepts about
glass.*

F

Sherry Schmidt
KNOTTED CONTAINER #7
Double half-hitch
knotting with linen, wool
and sisal; 19 by 15 by 15
inches.

B
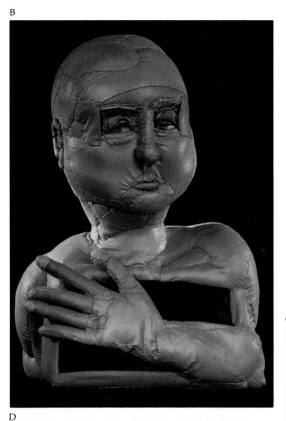

A
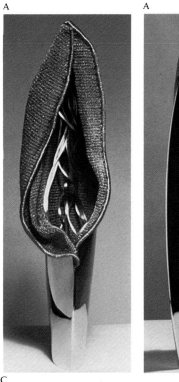

A

C

D

E

F
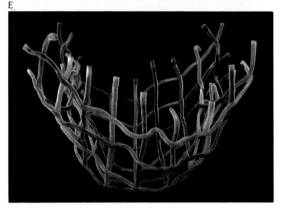

G

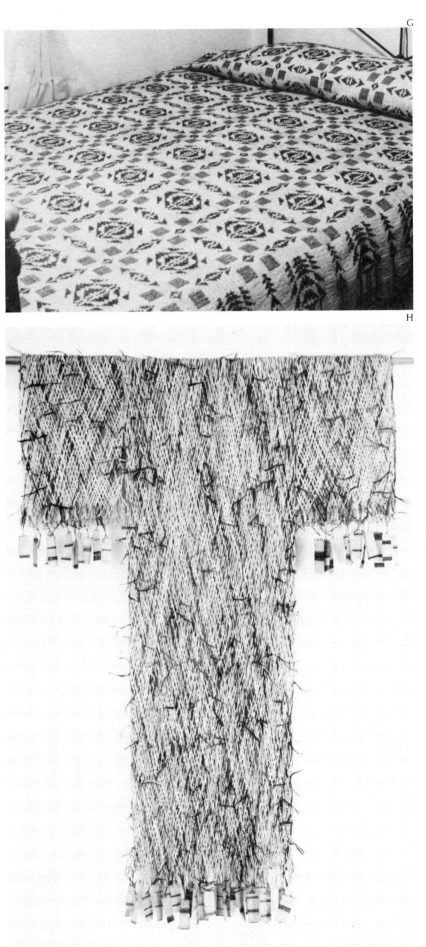

G
Loris Connolly
SUMMER/WINTER COVERLET
Summer/winter weave of
wool and cotton; double-
bed size.

H
Jan Janeiro
KIMONO FORM #2
Needle woven raffia,
plaited and resist-dyed;
40 by 50 inches.

I
Lillian Elliott
WIND
Twining and binding
with reed, linen and
wood stripping; 11 by 34
by 10 inches.

H

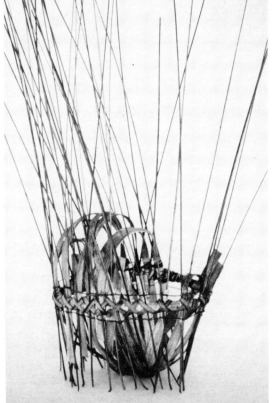

I

A
Terry Pommett
UNTITLED
Reed and cane; 13 by 13
by 13 inches.

B
Kari Lønning
A.J.'S ARROW
Rattan; 4 rod waling; 18
by 3 inches.

*Working within a functional
context, my aim is to design
baskets which are as visually
strong as they are structurally
sound.*

C
Jane Sauer
WOMAN BASKET
Linen; basketry figure-
eight knotting and
wrapping; 10 by 12½ by
9 inches.

*I am trying to use basketry
techniques to express sculptural
forms, using nature as my
generator, therefore getting
pure forms with the softness of
natural fibers.*

A

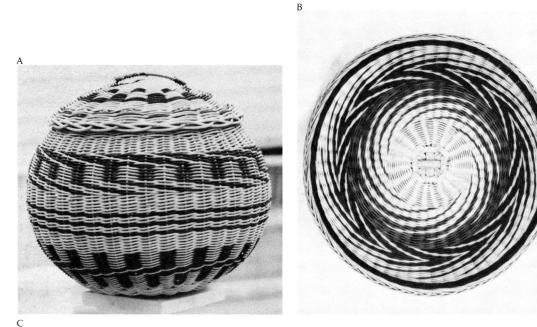

C

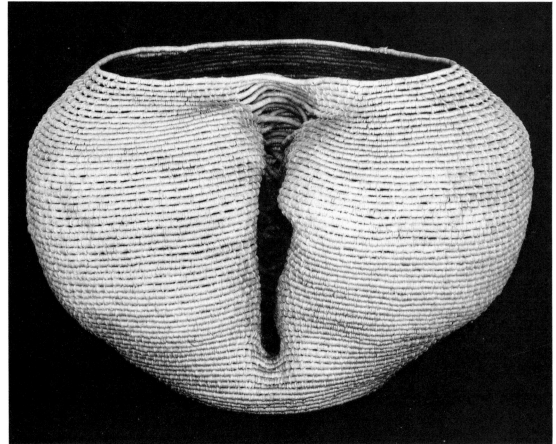

D

Catherine J. Ingebretsen
WHEAT
Flat reed, cane and half-round reed; plaited with inlay and colored with wood stain; 13 by 13 by 2 inches. Photo by Faith Anderson.

E
Carol Shaw-Sutton
CROSSING
Raffia; coiled; 18 by 13 inches.

F
Hisako Sekijima
TEE-TWINING OPEN WORK BASKET
Willow rattan; 17½ by 7½ inches. Photo by Bob Hanson.

D

E

F

A
Jane Sauer
SCORPIO
Wrapped silk and waxed
cotton; half-hitch knot
forms the body of the
basket; 3 by 3 by 7½
inches.

B
Susan Anderson
UNTITLED
Plaited tapes made from
commercial cotton
blends; 24 by 24 by 5
inches.
*I am primarily interested in
exploring the interaction of
color through changes in
juxtaposition.*

C
Cynthia Porter
UNTITLED
Loom-woven wool,
cotton, metallic and wire;
18 by 30 by 36 inches.
*In this balanced form, I was
interested in dealing with
movements and transparencies
—a form which would not be
ruled by the materials, or the
force of gravity.*

D
Gary Trentham
SWISS LINEN BASKET
Coiled linen with linen
braids added; 32 inch
diameter, 9 inches tall.

A

B

C

D

E
Roxy Ross Mosteller
BEOWULF
Polypropelene cord, knotted in double half-hitch; 20 by 8 by 13 inches.

Beowulf is an abstraction of the kind of helmet that could have been worn by this hero. The mask was loosely based on the Sutton Hoo helmet found in England, and made about 500 A.D.

F
Candy Miller
UNTITLED
Knotted jute; 32 by 14 by 4 inches.

G
Dorothy Gill Barnes
FIBER RELIEF WITH FERN STEMS
Fern stems wet-woven into a mixed warp of linen, raffia and rayon; 8 by 11 by 2 inches.

All my work, both on and off the loom, begins with natural materials gathered and cured.

H
Ellen Fanger Dickinson
WHITE SPIRAL GROUP
Figure-eight basketry stitch with wool and polished jute; largest piece—6 by 9 inches.

E

E

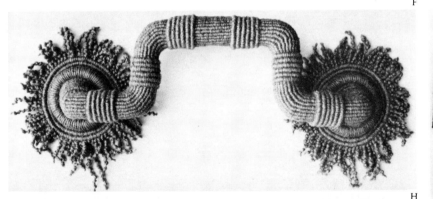

F

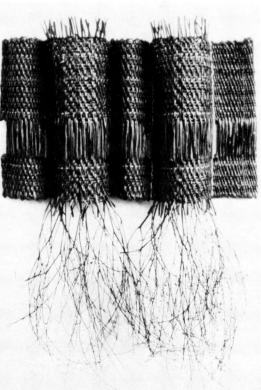

G

H

A

Karen Stoller

LIVID WHITE
Handwoven and wrapped
silk, alpaca and mohair;
21 by 21 by 4 inches.

B

Grace Hamilton

TRIAD
Needleweaving over
round reed with wool;
mounted on walnut
pedestal, handmade by
artist; 14 by 16 by 19
inches.

*After several years of working
in the area of stitchery and
tapestry weaving, I began to
experiment with off-loom
weaving techniques that would
allow my fiber to grow and
move, swell and undulate.
Using molded round reed as a
warp allows me to design
pieces which have several
planes emerging within one
space. My work is highly
influenced by the gentle
shadows and contours of the
New Mexico landscape.*

C

**Karon Hagemeister-
Winzenz**

ARTIFACTS #1
Wool, cotton, quills,
handwoven tapestry
treated with acid and
bleach, wrapped found-
objects; 11 by 23 by 3
inches.

*I have always been fascinated
by certain aspects of decay and
by the ephemeral quality of
physical matter.*

D

Janice Lessman

INTERVALS III
Felted and handwoven
linen, wool, aluminum; 6
by 14 by 7 inches.

A

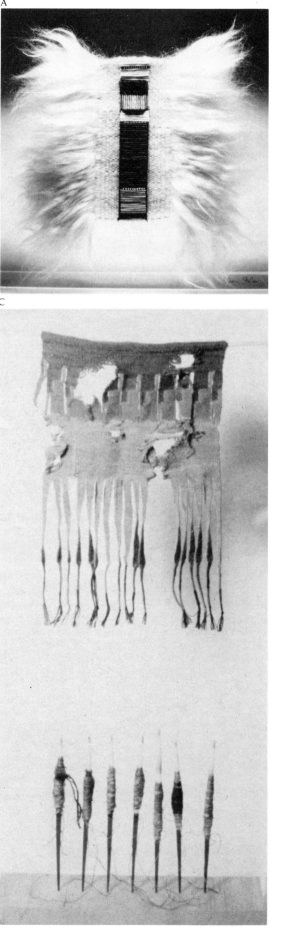

B

C

D

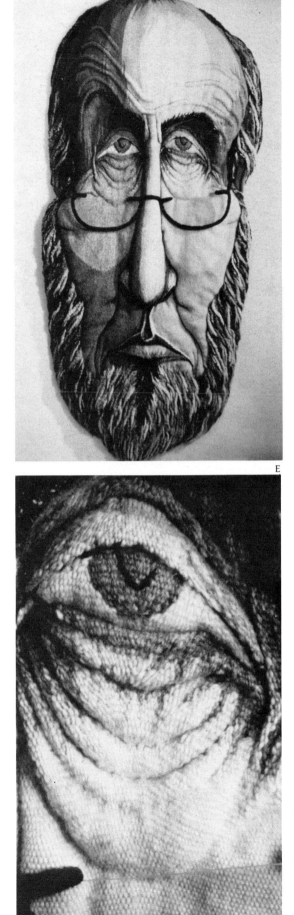

E

E

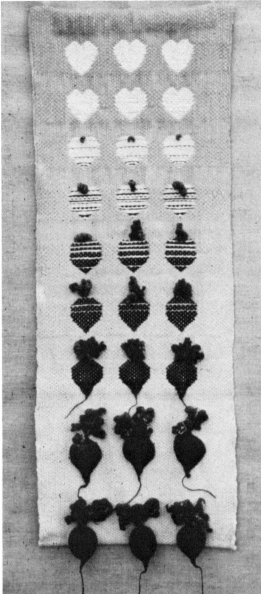

F

Penny J. Rupley
SKEPTICISM
Wool and wool blends,
handwoven flat and hand
stitched with crochet and
trapunto; 39 by 87 by 8
inches.

*Bernard Berenson said, "A
great painter really does not
need more than a face. If he
possesses the power of making
a face expressive, he can make
it say anything." This reflects
the goal to which I aspire—to
express the varying aspects of
the human condition, as
perceived through my eyes.
The imagery in my fiber faces
is a reflection of my own
observations and intuitions—
exploration of these feelings is
an integral part of my daily
life, and I am continually
making sketches and taking
notes for future reference.*

F
Joyce Marquess
HEARTBEETS
Wool and rayon, multi-
harness weave with
crochet; 16 by 36 inches.

*I've been using hearts in my
work for a long time—and I'm
very fond of puns!*

G
Hideho Tanaka
SQUARE #1
Cotton, wood; 3 by 3 by
2 feet.

G

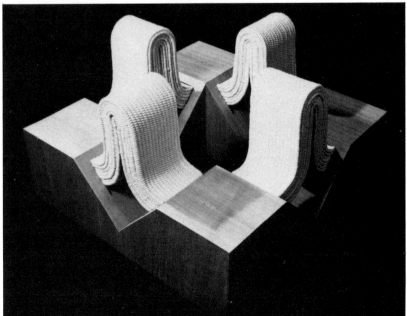

A
Cynthia Gale Nosek
MATILDA
Crocheted wool, mohair over a wire armature; 36 by 36 by 31 inches.

I crocheted MATILDA to prove that crochet not only lends itself to abstract, soft sculpture, but can also be used to create a realistic, life-sized human figure. Using various white wools, I began to crochet over a frame, molded from armature wire. 1000 hours later, MATILDA was completed and the yarn had taken on a life of its own.

B
George H. Brett
SEE SAW
Machine and hand knitting with 4-ply cotton twine (tobacco twine); installation 14 by 20 by 24 feet.

The idea of negative space has always been one that I've enjoyed playing with. I first explored this in my black and white photography, then translated it when I started working with knotted spider webs. The webs brought attention to two-dimensional spaces that had been previously taken for granted: the open space between two branches of a tree or between two buildings. This feeling is perhaps the primary emphasis of my work: the utilization of "empty space" in such a way that it is not filled, nor does it remain empty.

C
Martha Stein
CHRYSALIS
Pulled warp modules of cotton, silk and synthetic fibers, woven on a frame loom; 37 by 15 (diameter) inches. Photo by Robert E. Barrett.

A

A
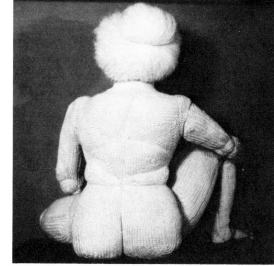

B

C

D
Pamela E. Becker
WOVEN STRUCTURE
Pulled warp weaving of
raffia and Swiss straw;
18 by 18 by 16 inches.

E
Jon B. Wahling
LINE ENVIRON
Shaped, plain woven
linen with aluminum; six
elements, each 82 by 102
by 12 inches. Photo by D.
R. Goff-Quicksilver.

D

C

E

A

Donvieve Calabrese
CHAIR
Wool, jute; star tapestry
hand spun and shaped to
fit armature; 75 by 86 by
48 inches.

B

Sharron Parker
WINDOW/CEILING PANELS
Cotton canvas, stuffed; 6
by 24 by 2½ feet.

*This work was commissioned,
in part, to keep heat from
escaping through the large
windows . . . and it works!*

C

Norma Minkowitz
THE LANDSCAPE OF MY MIND
Cotton, synthetic fibers,
dacron, muslin; crochet,
knit, trapunto, applique.
32½ by 28½ by 5½
inches.

D

Elizabeth S. Gurrier
HE
Floor cushion of
unbleached muslin;
quilting, trapunto, hand
and machine stitched;
seat—16 by 16 by 12
inches, back—28 inches
high.

A

B

C

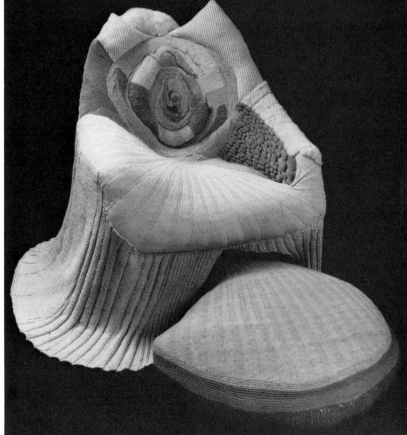

D

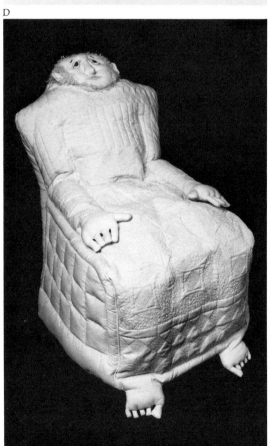

74

STITCHED
PRESSED
& PIECED

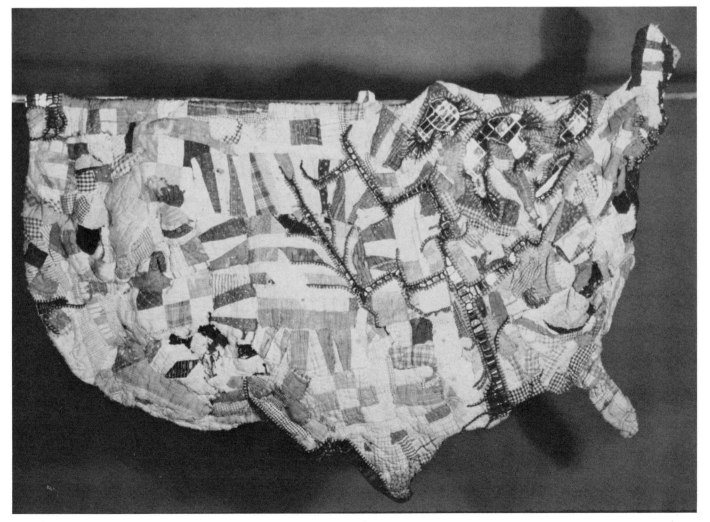

overleaf

Jeanne Whitty
OLD GLORY
Scraps from an old red, white and blue quilt, mirrors, vegetable dyed yarns; stitchery and stuffed applique; 60 by 24½ inches. Photo by Anne Miller.

A
Anne B. Morrell
BIRDS IN FLIGHT
Machine appliqued and hand quilted wall hanging of cotton blends; 58 by 70 inches.
I am a painter and seamstress. I began to combine my two interests into quilting five years ago, after I saw a show of quilts at the Whitney Museum in New York.

B
Patricia Flauto
A SERIES OF IMAGINARY COMPOSITIONS
Machine quilted cotton, silk-screened using torn paper stencils and Colortex textile pigments; 80 by 120 inches.

C
Leslie Fuller
EVEREST FROM TYANBOCHE
Machine applique and hand quilting with cotton, satin and ribbon; 96 by 110 inches.

A

B

C

D

Francoise Barnes
ETUDES DE COURBES
Wall quilt of machine pieced and hand quilted cottons and cotton blends; 73 by 75 inches.

I would like to cover mountains, meadows and rivers, the Empire State Building and the island of Cyprus with quilts, preferably mine . . .

E

Margot Strand Jensen
YARD QUILT
Cotton, mono-printed, versatex pigments; hand pieced and hand quilted; 64 by 78 inches.

This is a bittersweet quilt. Upon learning that I was to move from my beloved environment of the Blue Ridge Mountains of Virginia, to the dry and dusty plains of Colorado, I decided to make a memory quilt. I picked all the plant materials used to print the fabric from my yard or along my road where all of this greenery grew lush.

F

B. Leigh Herndon
GARDEN QUILT I
Dye painting with fiber reactive dye on cotton flannel; quilted; 78 by 90 inches.

Mary Lou Smith
CHRYSANTHEMUM
Hand quilted wall
hanging of cotton, cotton
blends and muslin; hand
and machine pieced; 68
by 68 inches. Photo by
Nancy Halpern.

*This piece was originally
conceived as pure geometric
design, but when completed, it
seemed reminiscent of a giant
football mum. The circular
quilting stitches create motion
in the design.*

B
Marie Wilson
REPRISE
Applique, patchwork,
machine quilting, hand
and machine embroidery;
with assorted fabrics; 5
by 5 feet.

C
Adelaide Winstead
LITURGICAL SETTING FOR A
FESTIVE CELEBRATION OF
THE HOLY EUCHARIST AT
EASTER
Silk, cotton and polyester
fabrics, appliqued and
machine stitched; altar
front—40 by 61 inches.

A

B

C

D

Judith Stein
UNTITLED
Etching on cotton;
trapunto, channel
quilting; 80 by 80 inches.

*This quilt was done using
traditional printmaking
techniques (etching on a zinc
plate, etching ink and a press),
applied to fabric, rather than
paper. It produces a more
three-dimensional result than
is possible on paper.*

E

Helen W. Richards
AT AUTUMN'S END
Hand quilted and
appliqued wool, rayon
challis and resist dyed
velveteen; 46 by 40
inches.

F

Nancy E. Rial
POCKET QUILT #1
Machine pieced and
quilted velveteen and
satin; 78 by 84 inches.

*The velveteen background looks
dark from the left side, light
from the right. The slashes of
satin go from dark at the top to
light at the bottom. This combination creates special effects
as you move by the piece.*

E

F

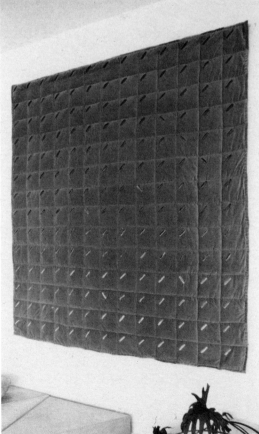

A

Carol Lawrence-Thompson
STUFFED TUBE QUILT
Cotton and cotton blended corduroy, chinos and plain weave fabrics; 84 by 100 inches.

B

Elaine Plogman
MAGNOLIA
Hand and machine pieced and hand quilted cotton blends; 53 by 80 inches.
I am a weaver-turned-stitcher. That is why my patchwork pieces are seldom developed from a quilt block, but are conceived as a whole design, or in strips.

C

Ruth E. Woodbury
BICYCLE TRIP
Quilted wall hanging of cotton and cotton blends; machine and hand stitched with laid-on quilting done by hand; 34 by 35 inches.

D

Nancy Crow
Velma Brill
JANUARY II
Cotton/polyester broad-cloth; designed and strip-pieced by Nancy Crow; hand quilted by Velma Brill; 80 by 80 inches.
I am a full-time studio artist producing contemporary quilts. I am concerned with the piecing, as I am not a quilter and therefore must find someone else to do that part for me. The piecing, though tedious, is the creative part for me and a pieced top reflects my inner growth, turmoil, dreams, likes and dislikes.

C

A

E
Helen Bitar
UNTITLED
Seminole piece work with cotton and corduroy; 41 by 55 inches.

F
Elaine Plogman
QUILTED RYA
Machine pieced and hand quilted cotton, synthetics, velveteen and wool; 76 by 60 inches.

G
Nancy Smith
THROUGH COLORED WINDOWS
Quilted cotton and satin; 62 by 98 inches.

D

E

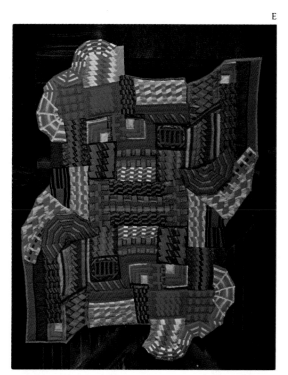

F

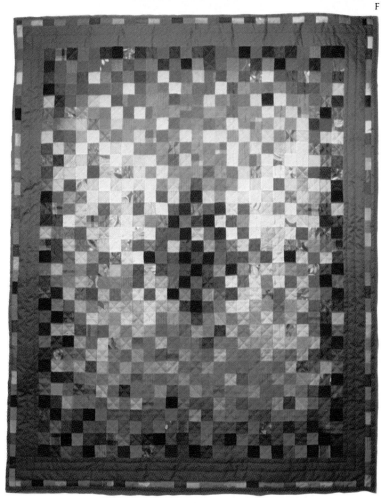

G

81

A
Jean Kamins
SPAGHETTI EATERS
Fabric applique; 42 by 48
inches.

B
Margaret Sherman
WHORES
Machine stitchery on
muslin; 24 by 26 inches.
*I draw on muslin, using my
sewing machine as a child
might use a crayon on paper.*

A

C
Molly R.-M. Fowler
THE WEDDING
Hand dyed and handspun
wool, silk, mohair, ramie;
woven and felted; 27 by
40 inches.

*Almost all my works are
commissioned—about ten per
year. This means that I
respond to the client's needs,
tastes, and the eventual site.
While this imposes obvious
limits, it also encourages
growth and change.*

D
Margot Strand Jensen
DRESS-UP PILLOWCASE
Satin, mono-printed
using transfer process
with a copier; machine
quilted; 32 by 23 inches.

*The little girl in each
photograph is me, at the age of
five. I remember the evening
well—two Homecoming
princesses, one Homecoming
queen, and I (the university's
mascot), all lined up for the
traditional photos in front of a
full auditorium of spectators. I
remember my jealous feelings
at that time—how I wanted to
be the queen and hold the
bouquet of flowers. Now,
through my symbolic, childish
demeanings to the queen and
princesses, I can get a laugh
out of those immature emotions
. . . and hopefully, so can
others!*

C

D

D

A

Nancy Crow
Mrs. Levi Troyer
NEWE IV
Cotton/polyester broad-
cloth; designed and strip
pieced by Nancy Crow;
hand quilted by Mrs. Levi
Troyer; 80 by 80 inches.

*I think every artist who
succeeds (in their own terms)
has some ability to keep
moving forward in the face of
constant obstacles . . .
emotional, mental, financial,
physical, and that is what sets
them apart from all the ones
who have tried and quit, and
from those who always talk
about trying or starting, but
never get beyond the talking
stage.*

B

Esther Parkhurst
DIAMOND DIVISION
Machine pieced and hand
quilted cotton fabrics; 48
by 48 inches.

*My inspiration comes from an
interest in and love for early
American, pieced quilts.
However, I make an effort not
to repeat the traditional quilt
look, but rather concentrate on
producing my personal images,
while using the traditional
technique.*

C

Sharon Sharp
MOONLIT LANDSCAPE
Machine pieced and hand
quilted cotton and cotton
blends; 72 by 96 inches.

A

B

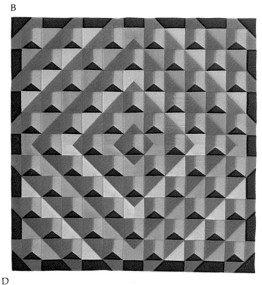

D

C

E

D
Pat Cairns
SECRET SEA
Machine pieced and
quilted satin and cotton;
50 by 62 inches.

E
Michael James
AURORA
Cotton, satin, velveteen;
hand pieced and hand
quilted; 96 by 108 inches.

F
Leslie Fuller
PARROT QUILT
Machine applique,
trapunto and hand
quilting on satin and
watered silk; 96 by 110
inches.

G
Judith Dingle
ROSE MAROC
Cotton and cotton
blends, pieced and
quilted; 60 by 90 inches.
Photo by Michael Sheba.

F

G

Martha Opdahl
SARABANDA
Machine quilting and
trapunto on kettlecloth;
60 by 60 inches.
*I am interested in rendering
my designs through contrast in
texture, rather than contrast in
color. Off-white enhances the
play of light and shadow, and
the ridging, raised areas
produced by the cording and
padding give the designs a bas
relief sculptural quality.*

B

**Margaret Stephenson
Coole**
MOTHER AND CHILD
Trapunto and cording on
unbleached cotton; 9 by
18 by 2 inches.
*This is my translation of a
Hittite stone relief, 800 BC.*

C

Analee Reutlinger
DANDELION #2
Trapunto on silk,
mounted on a muslin
backing and colored with
acrylic paint; 40 by 45
inches.
*For years I did this type of
work, calling it "stuffed
drawings". Then in the early
70's, I was astonished to come
across the "trapunto" technique
in a craft book—to rediscover
the fact that whatever it is
you're doing, someone, at some
time, has probably already
done it!*

A

C

B

D
Ellen J. Zahorec
BLACK AND WHITE
AMERICAN SAMPLER
Stitchery on handmade
paper; 20 by 22 inches.

E
Elizabeth S. Gurrier
SINGLE ANGEL
Unbleached muslin,
cheesecloth; embroidery,
quilting, trapunto,
machine and hand
stitched; 21 by 60 inches.
*Unbleached muslin is pure and
simple—it doesn't get in the
way of the design. Without
color, and the emotional
response that it brings, the
design itself must do the
communicating.*

F
Patricia Malarcher
OMMATIDIA
Mylar (silver, gold,
copper) on a linen
backing with machine
and hand stitching and
applique; 48 by 48 by 3
inches.
*My hope in this piece was to
have the reflective quality of
mylar function as an active
design element. The basic unit
is a square consisting of two
concentric pyramids; one
concave, the other convex, with
different colors on adjacent
forms. The slant of the sides
allows the colors to interact,
creating a third color. The
units are organized to suggest
a diagonal streak of light
across the piece.*

D

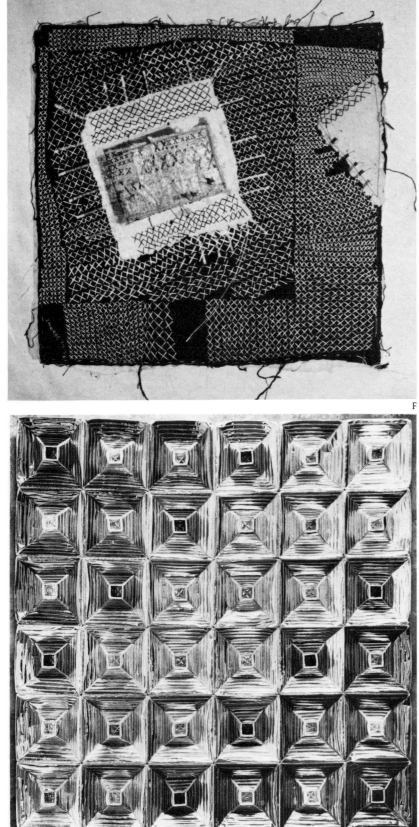

E

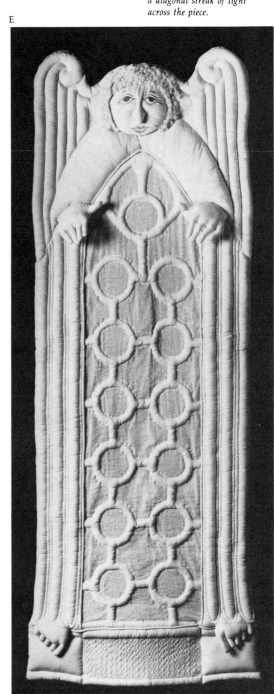

F

87

A
Judith Dingle
ORANGE BECOMING RED
SERIES #1
Cotton and cotton
blends, pieced and
quilted; 53 by 53 inches.
Photo by Michael Sheba.

*I am interested in optical
effects using geometric design,
bas-relief quilting, and color to
give the two-dimensional
surface three-dimensional
qualities. I often use the
expressive qualities of color
spectrums to emphasize change
and movement across the piece.*

B
Esther Parkhurst
CROSS WITH SHELL
Cotton fabrics; hand
applique and piece work;
hand and machine
stitched; hand quilted; 49
by 49 inches.

C
Elizabeth Lady
KOI
Machine stitched and
embroidered polyester
crepe-back satin and
muslin; 21 by 7½ by 4
inches.

*Koi means carp. I was
happy to discover crepe-
back satin, which conveys
the soft shimmer of fish in
motion. Also happy to
discover that closely-
stitched fabric (fins and
tail) has much more body.*

D
Chris Dydo
OLD JEANS THAT NO ONE
WEARS
Denim wall quilt; 48 by
67 inches.

*With old jeans (and new ones
that never fit), I made this
quilt to hang next to my bed to
keep the cold air from seeping
through an uninsulated wall!
The pattern is my own
variation of the "windmill"
block.*

A
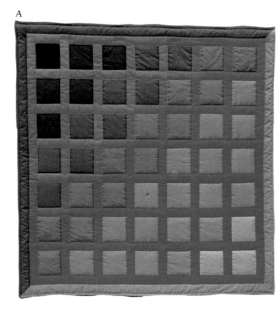

B

C

D

E

F

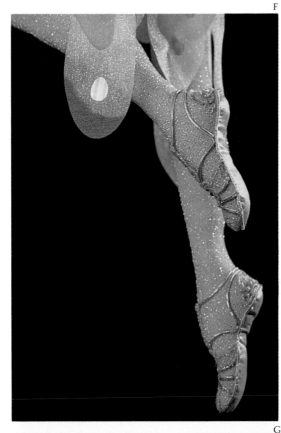

F

E
Rhoda R. Cohen
SOUVENIR OF MAINE
Wall quilt of cotton and cotton blends, hand quilted and appliqued; 7 by 5 feet.

F
Marilyn Serra
BUTTERFLY WOMAN
Applique and trapunto with silk, satin, muslin, sequins and beads; 12 by 24 by 7 inches.

Since childhood I've been fascinated with dolls, puppets, fairy tales and costumes—the more elaborate and fantasy-like, the more exciting. Often I am attracted to a fabric which inspires a piece, as in the case of BUTTERFLY WOMAN. *On seeing the iridescent fabric (wings), I immediately thought of an ethereal figure with shimmering wings.*

G
Jo-Ellen Trilling
EARTHBOUND
Silk, rayon, stocking, felt; 44 by 84 by 48 inches.
Photo by Bob Hanson.

G

G

A
Suellen Glashausser
FOUR STITCHED PAPER
TOWELS
Paper, thread; 10 by 10
inches each.
*Embellishment of the throw-
away—glorification of
overlooked, everyday
materials . . .*

B
Susanna E. Lewis
BOBBIN LACE WITH
HORSESHOE CRABS
Linen lace thread,
horseshoe crab shells;
Russian braid (tape style)
lace; 14 by 14½ inches.
*I have written about, and
taught traditional lacemaking
techniques, and their
application to contemporary
design. I chose this particular
style of bobbin lace to amplify
the perfect symmetry and
delicacy of the molted "baby"
shells of the ancient horseshoe
crab.*

C
Kathi Ince
KITE HANGING
Muslin and cheesecloth,
hand stained with acrylic;
36 by 60 inches.

A

B

C

D
Joanna Slater
SUNDAY REVIEW - 2
Hand stitchery on a
printed cotton back-
ground; 23 by 15 inches.

E
Myrna Shiras
THOUGHTFUL GIFT BOX
Handmade papers, hand
stitched with cotton and
silk threads; 16 by 14
inches.

F
Patricia Flauto
EXCESS
Loom-shaped, woven
cotton; pleated and
stitched; 10 by 20 inches.
*I did a series of these pieces in
order to break away from the
limitations of the loom. I tried
to minimize time spent at the
loom and spend more time
creating the finished piece.
Collage suited this aim.*

D

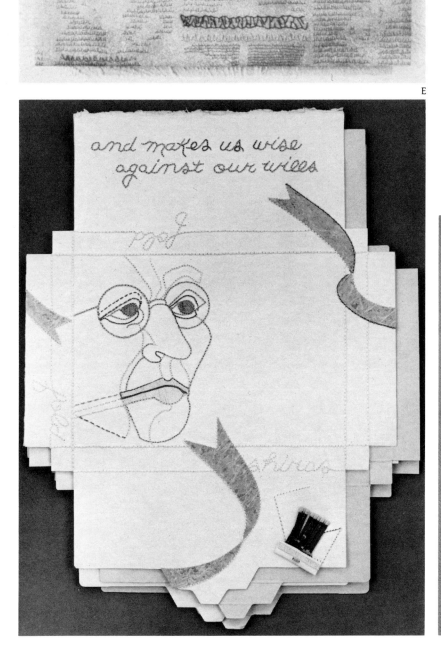

E

F

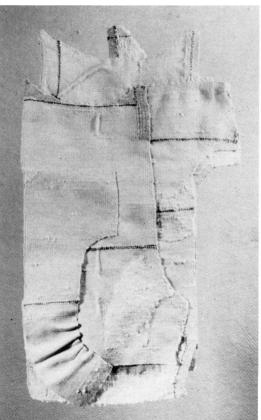

Barbara L. Smith
SPRING RAIN
Machine stitched silk,
cotton and cotton/rayon
blends which have been
sprayed with inko dyes;
24 by 24 inches.

B

Lucy A. Jahns
UNTITLED
Stuffed, knotless netting;
16 by 12 inches.

C

Barbara Allen Wagner
CHAPEL OF GRACE ALTAR
RUG, PRIE DIEUX AND
HASSOCKS
Basketweave with
Paternayan wool on 10-
gauge Zwiegart canvas;
rug—8 by 18 feet; prie
dieux—10 by 15 by 6
inches; hassock—8 by 20
by 6 inches. Photo by
Diane Beeston.

*I was commissioned to design
canvas works for the Grace
Cathedral's Chapel of Grace. I
took patterns directly from
architectural motifs found in
the chapel and the Great Rose
Window in the cathedral. All
of the work was executed by
embroiderers from the
Northern California Episcopal
Diocese.*

A

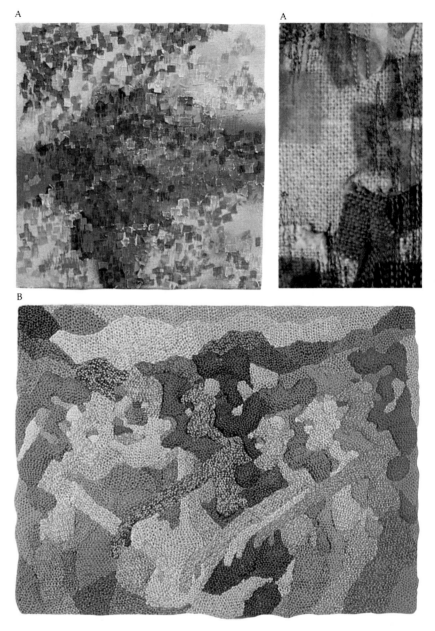

B

C

D

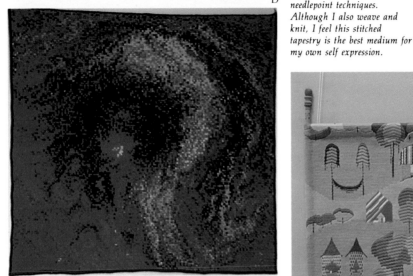

D

Paulette Peroni
COSMOS III
Long stitch embroidery with wool on canvas; 5 by 5 feet.

I started making tapestries 12 years ago, using this particular technique of embroidery. The long stitch allows the wool to better capture light than classic needlepoint techniques. Although I also weave and knit, I feel this stitched tapestry is the best medium for my own self expression.

E

Joan Wolfer
CAMP AT 3:30
Needlework on canvas with wool and cotton yarns; 42 by 20 inches.

F

James Williams
NOAH'S ARK
Rug; basketweave and tent stitch needlepoint with Persian and tapestry wool yarns; 31 by 59 inches.

G

Rhona Golfman Shapiro
UNTITLED
Wool, cheesecloth and wooden beads on canvas which is stained with herbs, teas, etc.; 43½ by 72 inches.

This wall hanging began as two separate pieces of canvas stretched onto frames. After staining them and working in the wool, beads and cheesecloth, I cut the canvases into six strips and stitched them together.

E

F

G

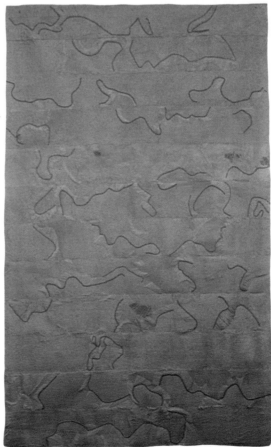

93

A

Kathy Constantinides
INTIMATION
Layered weaving of
pellon with metal
washers and cable; 13 by
13 by 1 inches.

The primary references for my
work are time and layers
which I see in nature: the
Grand Canyon, seacoasts, the
rain forest, archaeological
finds. The deposits of ages
result in layers. The building-
up process reverses itself
through erosion and
excavation. As enduring and
tough as nature seems, in
reality it is vulnerable,
mutable.

B

Joanne Mattera
RED LINE DRAWING 5
Oil pastel on Mexican
bark paper with hand
stitched and knotted
linen thread; 11 by 15
inches.

C

Lida Gordon
CONNECTIONS
Silk; 10 by 28 by 2½
inches.

A

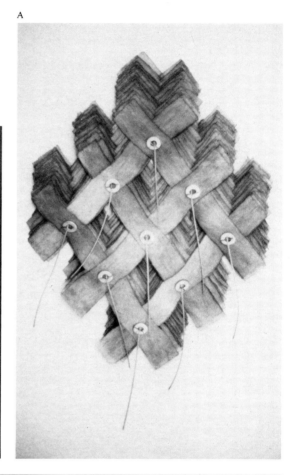

B

C

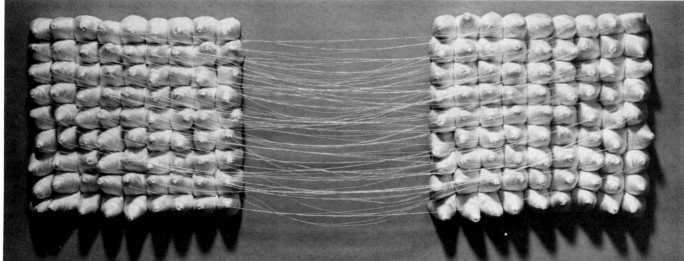

D

D
Beverly Plummer
THREE PLANS FOR A GARDEN
Handmade paper of
fibers from corn stalks
and shucks; 28 by 12¼
inches.

*The plants are reduced to a
pulp, dispersed in water, and
then gathered together on a
screen to form sheets.*

E
Christine Mesarch
FOOLED AGAIN
Fabric applique; 72 by 48
inches.

*I'm a painter and this piece is
one of my favorites because it
inspired several paintings after
it was completed.*

F
Barbara Murak
UNTITLED
Embroidery with yarn,
thread and assorted
fibers on a linen-type
fabric; 27 by 36 inches.

*My approach to fiber design
has always been free,
somewhat experimental,
spontaneous and instinctive,
depending upon my mood. My
designs are not something I
think about or sketch
beforehand . . . they develop as
I go along.*

E

F

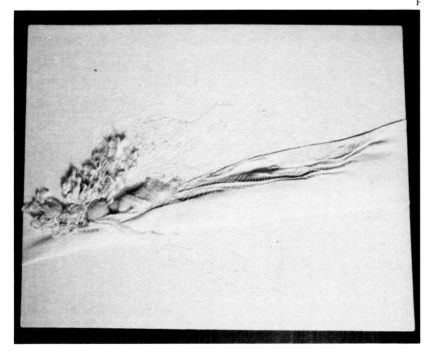

A

Felix and Emma Senger
ICON
Applique and machine
embroidery on assorted
fabrics; 68 by 60 inches.

*We came to this country from
Germany in 1959 and
designed and executed stained
glass works for churches. Our
first commission for a wall
hanging came in 1970, and
we have completed many since
that time, including this one
for the Church of the
Byzantine Rite.*

B

Virginia Jacobs
FLOWERBIRD
Cotton, cotton blends
with quilting, applique,
beading and Xerography;
60 by 32 inches. Photo by
Tom Bernard.

*This wall hanging is an
attempt to express the
marvelous and uniquely
inventive American ethnic
juxtapositions in a formalized
context.*

C

Amy Zerner
THE MAGIC OF FINDHORN
Sculptural collage of
assorted fabrics, beads,
mirrors and handmade
antique items; 40 by 78
inches.

*The legend of Findhorn
concerns a windswept Scottish
moor, transformed into an
Eden-like garden through the
power of faith in Pan. This
legend appeals to me because of
my own belief in the powers of
the mind.*

A

A

B

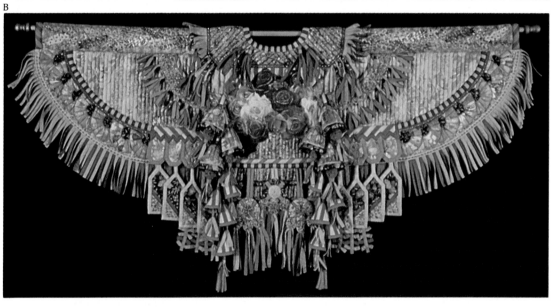

C

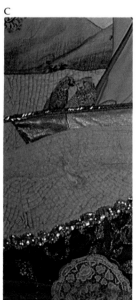

C

D
Ruth E. Woodbury
SCANDAL IN THE MOSQUE
Quilted wall hanging of
cotton and cotton blends;
machine and hand
stitched patchwork and
applique; 46 by 76 inches.

*I work with a group of
quilters who share fabrics and
ideas. Each person works on
her own quilt except in the
"sandwich" phase when we
baste the batting and lining to
the top in a joint effort.*

E
Francoise Barnes
EYES OF ISIS
Hand quilted cottons and
cotton blends; center
medallions and most of
the hexagons are strip
pieced; 76 by 76 inches.

F
Janet Higgins
LOST
Handmade felt on taffeta
with silk and metallic
threads, sequins, ribbon
and plastic flowers;
applique and trapunto; 16
by 24 inches.

*The wall hangings that I do
are very autobiographical,
coming from strong, emotional
experiences. These emotions get
filtered through a very formal
design structure—perhaps in
an attempt to de-sentimentalize
them. Rather than raw
emotion spread across the
surface, I want to present an
elegant image—much the way
one must restrain one's actual
emotions in real life,
presenting a more controlled
and contained image to the
world.*

D

E

F

A
Jeannie M. Spears
DEAR HOUSEWIFE
Brushed nylon tricot;
heat-transfer print, T-
shirt iron-ons; hand
quilted; 80 by 96 inches.

B
Debra Millard
COUNTERPOINT
Hand dyed cotton muslin
using Procion dye,
machine pieced, hand
quilted; 90 by 76 inches.

*I use a computerized WEAVE
program to explore various
patterns. A quilt block module
is defined, and then "woven"
across the page. This allows
me to see many pattern
alternatives in a matter of
minutes.*

C
**Margaret Stephenson
Coole**
ROSE WINDOW
Wall quilt with batik
inserts, cathedral window
quilting technique on
cotton; 35 by 35 inches.

*This piece was inspired by the
name of the technique along
with a vivid memory I have of
the rose window in the
Chartres Cathedral in France.*

B
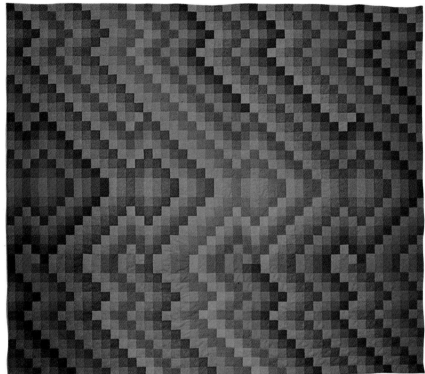

A

C

D

C
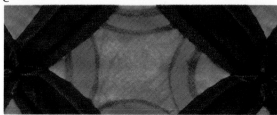

D
Pat Rutledge
DAY DREAMS, NIGHT
DREAMS
Quilted cotton print cloth
with Miyako dyes; 30 by
32 inches.

E
Linda McFarland
VESTIGIAL POCKETS #722
Applique with dyed
gauze;
20 by 24 by 1 inches.
*For some time I have been
interested in pockets—
historically, physically and
conceptually.*

F
**Nora Hutchinson
Johnson**
SILK WINDOW
Thai silks, padded and
stitched to industrial felt;
27 by 36 inches.

G
Lee A. Grzelak
FRACTURED APPROACH
Raw silk, embroidery
floss; 16 by 14 by 1
inches.
*I am an artist who has always
worked in fiber, but am most
interested in art image. I am
aware that as images change,
other media might be more
appropriate. We in fiber must
not become so enamored with
technique that our art image
suffers.*

H
Georgia Donovan
STONE WALL
Handmade felt (wool);
dyed canvas; 4½ by 8
feet.
*In my felting work, I strive for
a rich build-up of color by
blending together many colors
of hand dyed fleece. I've had a
lot of fun with this piece, since
it always seems to draw
reactions and comments of
some kind.*

E

F

G

G

H

H

A
**Elizabeth Keatinge
Massie**
INTENSITY XXIII
Handmade papers
attached to linen; 18½ by
33¾ by 2 inches.

B
Anne Flaten Pixley
POST AND PAPER
SERIES 80-5
Handmade cotton paper;
5½ by 17 feet.

A

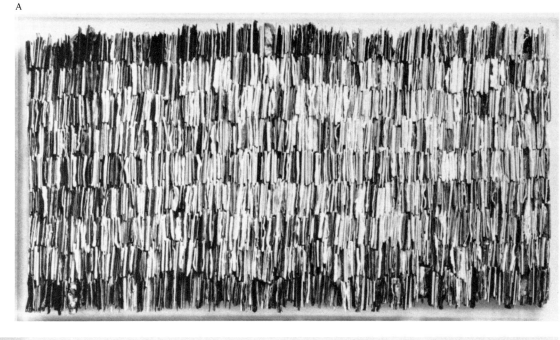

B

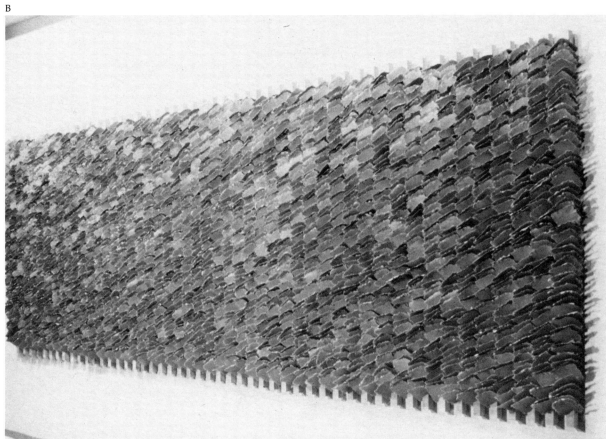

C
Atsuko Yamamoto
E NO ARU TEGAMI
European book-binding
technique using silk
cloth. Traditional
Japanese dyeing methods
and embroidery with
Japanese enamel thread.

D
Patricia Townsend
EXPANDING PLANES
Cast paper and waxed
linen; 32 by 35 by 8
inches.
*I enjoy strong geometric
multiple forms: triangles and
squares which have been set
into order, yet are acted upon
by gravity or other changes.*

E
Jesseca Ferguson
ANASAZI BOOK
Handmade paper (manila,
hemp and yucca), linen,
wood; 8 by 16 by 2
inches.
*This book is an exploration of
the meaning of fiber in the
lives of the Anasazi
"Basketmaker" Indians of the
Southwestern United States. It
is based on my work at the
Peabody Museum at Harvard.*

C

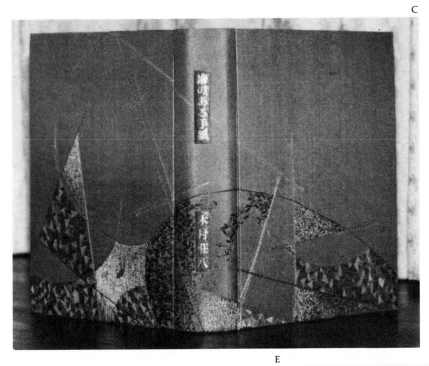

D

E

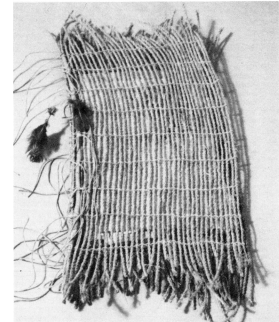

E

A

Eve N. Cotton

THE OLD ONE

Collage of dyed
newsprint, construction
paper, wrapping paper
and parchment; 18 by 24
inches.

*As a quilter, I have spent
much time piecing squares
together. After creating this
collage of paper shapes, I cut it
into squares and rearranged
them to create a unified, yet
random, piece.* THE OLD
ONE *looks to me like an
ancient textile fragment.*

B

Patricia Spencer

SMITH CREEK BACKDROP

Cyanotype printing on
handcast paper with
applique; 30 by 16 by 6
inches.

*This functions as a reminder
that wherever travels take
place, so do collections—we
function as space collectors.
Hence, small objects on the
surface.*

C

Neda AlHilali

PLEATED PIECE

Plaited, pleated, dyed,
pressed and painted rag
paper; 47 by 50 inches.

D

Constance Miller

FANTASY GARDENS
REVISITED II

Cotton, handmade paper,
raffia, reed, silk; Cushing
dye; 30 by 40 inches.

*My concerns and inspiration
come from landscapes and
suggestions of landscapes.*

A

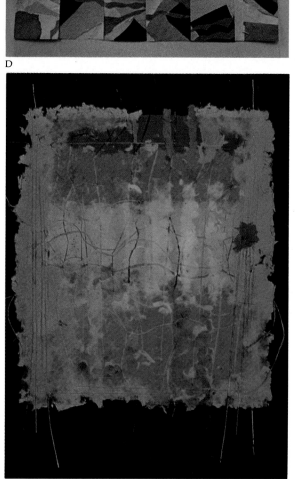

B

C

D

SURFACE
DESIGN

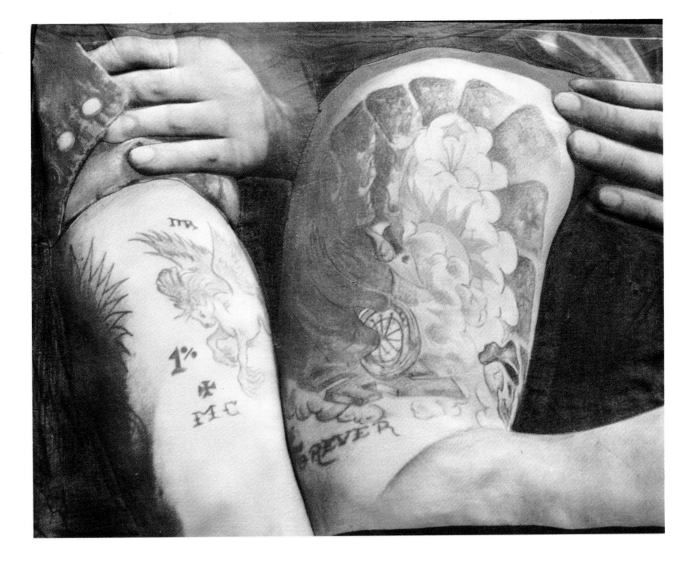

overleaf
Fern Helfand
TATOOED ARMS #2
Batik and trapunto on cotton with acrylics, colored pencils and Van Dyke brown print; 15 by 18 inches.

As a photographer, I have turned to textiles to achieve three-dimensional and tactile surfaces in my work. I try to bring the flat photographic image back to dimensional form as it existed in the world before the photograph was taken. The image is realized, however, in an altered and stylized state. I am also concerned with merging the process of photography and "art" with the traditional area of woman's craft in fiber.

A
Roberta Leahy
RUNNING STITCHES
Cotton broadcloth; West African resist dye technique (Alabere— "that which is sewn"); 44 by 70 inches.

The running stitches are sewn, drawn up tightly and then dyed.

B
Kathryn Edwards
UNTITLED
Textile paint on cotton canvas; 150 by 135 inches.

I am strongly influenced by my emotions—one day feeling as bold as these curtains, the next shy and totally intimidated by life. It took me four months just to make the curtains, but I loved every minute of it. They hang in the front room of my French Quarter apartment in New Orleans.

C
Cornelia Capwell Denker
DARWIN'S DREAM
Screen printed cotton, using a cut stencil technique with Britex dyes; 3 by 13 feet.

I tend to dream in repeats— perhaps Darwin did too!

A

B

C
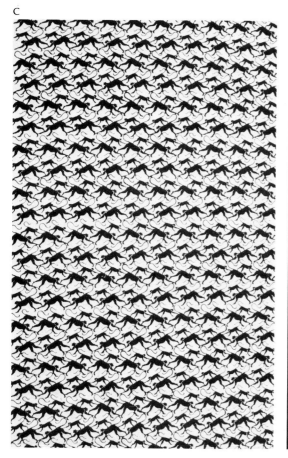

D

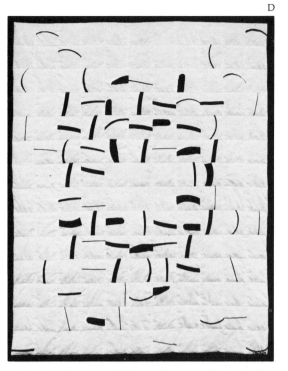

E

D
Anne B. Morrell
PLIE MANDARIN
Hand quilted wall
hanging of photo silk-
screened cotton blends;
62 by 50 inches.

E
Janis Gloystein
JAPANESE FAMILY CREST
QUILT
Cotton, silk-screened
with Versatex dye; 45 by
52 inches.
*This piece is a statement about
Japanese design—its
simplicity, asymmetrical
balance and order. It was
printed with a traditional
photo silk-screen technique and
pieced in a traditional manner,
but is not a traditional quilt.*

F
**Connie McEntire
Lehman**
SLIPPER SEARCH
Direct application of fiber
paint on cotton, quilted;
3 by 5 feet.

G
Dona Dowling Abt
MAGNOLIA GRANDIFLORA
Fiber reactive dyes on
cotton broadcloth; 15 by
22 inches.
*Japanese rice paste was
applied through a mulberry
paper stencil (Katazome), then
the cloth was dyed.*

F

G

A

Julie Kemble
FLORENTINE PERSUASION
French dyes on silk,
dacron and cotton velvet;
machine quilted; 50 by 50
inches.
*This was inspired by my
recent trip to Spain.*

B

Ofra Nadel
MIDNIGHT IRIS SCARF
Silk; alcohol-base dyes;
gutta resist; 36 by 36
inches.

A

B

C

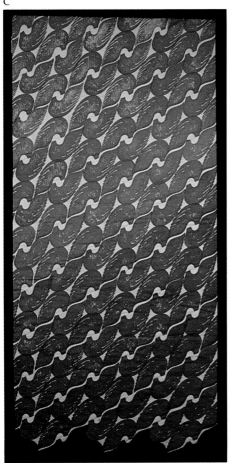

D

C
Anita Verstraete
WING
Quilted, block-printed
banner on cotton; 32 by
76 inches.

D
Madeline Liebling
SCARF
Cotton, photo silk-screen
printed with Procion dye;
26½ by 26½ inches.
*All my scarves are made to be
useful and beautiful—to take
real wear and tear by real
people.*

E
Sharla Jean Hoskin
RAIN
Silk-screened, channel
quilted cotton sateen and
rayon satin; 80 by 40 by
5 inches.

F
Christine Lardon-Rhone
YARILO 5
Batik; 76 by 59 inches.

G
Marian Clayden
HAND OF THE SUTTEE
Clamp resist, discharge
and dip dyed silk with
gold paint; 15 by 15
inches.
*This symbolic hand is an
expression of my horror at the
ancient rite of "suttee".
This tradition calls for the
widows of India to be burned
on the funeral pyre with their
dead husbands. On the way
to their death, they dipped a
hand in vermillion paint and
pressed it on stone—making
the stone sacred.*

H
Pat Grummet
LEPIDOPTERA ADOLESCENS
Smocking and tie-dye
with Perspex on silk; 27½
by 27½ by 2¾ inches.
*The sensuality of color and
touch, the fluidity of silk, the
repetition and rhythm of
pleating, the constriction of
binding in the tie-dye process;
the contrasts of hidden and
exposed areas, of hardness and
vulnerability . . . all have
analogies in the complex
existence of women.*

E

F

G

H

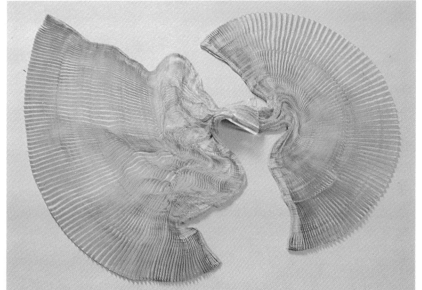

A
Mary Stieglitz
LOUVRE
Photograph on photo-
linen, stuffed and
stitched; 13 by 17 by 1
inches.
*My work results from the
integration of two areas of
expertise—photography and
textiles.*

B
Katharine Shearer
WATER LILY QUILT
Quilted batik with
Procion dyes on cotton;
40 by 40 inches.
*My husband and I have
worked with batik in our home
studio for years. We like the
freedom and self-direction that
this allows us.*

C
Karin Russo
UNTITLED
Cotton, silk-screened
with oil pastels; 16 by
17½ inches.

A

B

C

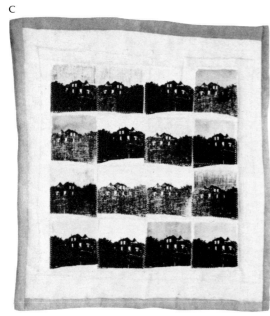

108

D

D
Dilys Stinson
CRUCIAN RUE
Wool tapestry; 86½ by 23½ inches.

E
Alice McClelland
SALUTE TO LOUIS LUMIERE
Cotton and silk; direct painted batik, Procion dyes; 92 by 104 by 1 inches.
I am trained as a painter and specialize in direct-painting batik processes. I like to make screens because the image goes through on both sides, and with this sheer cloth, each side is equally bright.

F
Kimberly Mason
UNTITLED
Dyed, pieced, painted and pleated cotton; 36 by 40 inches.

D

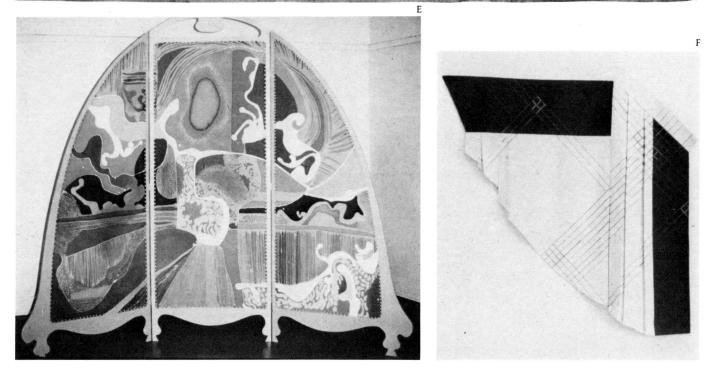

E

F

A

Mary Bero Nechvatal
DREAM DAZZLER
Muslin; fiber reactive
dyes; machine quilting;
96 by 96 inches.

*I read once that quilts were
only to be done in blues or
pastels—thought I'd create
nightmares (or inspiration)
under this one!*

B

Debra Millard
RASPBERRY DREAM II
Hand dyed cotton muslin,
machine pieced and
quilted; 40 by 40 inches.

C

Jacqueline Snyders
FLOWER QUILT II
Trapunto and quilting on
dye painted velveteen; 53
by 68 by 4½ inches.

D

Wenda F. von Weise
FABRICATED LANDSCAPE:
STRAIGHT FURROWS IN
GEOLOGIC TIME
Photo-screen prints on
silk, quilted; 73 by 80
inches.

B

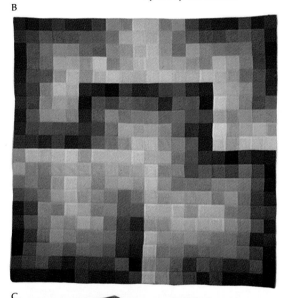

C

C

A

D

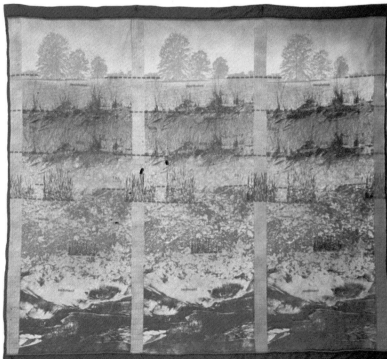

E

Dorothy McCuistion
SOFT FLAPS
Wool; felting; 42 by 54
by 3 inches. Photo by
John McCuistion.
*This was my first finished
attempt at felting. I love what
happens to the layers of felted
color when they are cut.*

F

Deborah Kaufman
CHAIR BY THE WINDOW
Handmade wool felt; 68
by 32 inches.

G

**Marleah Drexler
MacDougal**
DAWN
Layered felt; 55 by 30
inches.

H

Beatrice Moore
VEGETARIAN TROPHY SERIES:
FELTED PLUMAGE
Handmade, naturally
dyed felt, cotton canvas;
48 by 36 inches.

F

G

H

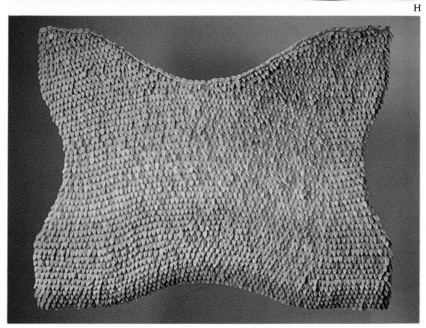

H

A

Jan Janeiro

IKAT FEATHERS #2

Shaped tapestry of linen, cotton and silk, with weft ikat and wrapping; 8 by 10 inches. Photo by Ted Macke.

B

Norma Rosen

NOW YOU SEE ME

Photo etching, trapunto, hand and machine embroidery on crepe satin; 14 by 7 by 3½ inches.

C

Kim Irwin

THE ICE AGE COMETH

Batik painting on cotton; 90 by 72 inches.

I am striving for simplification in my work as well as in my life. Simplicity is achieved when unnecessary elements are excluded; the vision is whole and critical analysis is not required. There is no message except for the visual elements to suggest an environment of fantasy and joy.

D

Cynthia Pannucci

FIGURATIVE LANDSCAPE

Patched, pieced and quilted Belgian cotton and cotton velveteen, silk-screened and hand painted with Procion dyes; 64 by 88 inches.

This quilt was made for a friend who was moving from Vermont to New York City. I wanted to combine hands and feet, designs she loved, with Vermont hillsides. If you view the quilt on the bed from either side, you see hills, which become large figures when viewed straight-on.

E

Carol L. Baker

REFERENCE WORK

Screen printed rayon challis, using fiber reactive dye, acrylic paint; hand quilted center with machine quilted and torn paper frame; 73 by 57 inches.

Since 1973 my work has been based primarily on the grid system, an attraction which I still do not fully understand.

REFERENCE WORK *began as a color study for fiber reactive dyes.*

F

Susan Pauley

TV SCREENS: DREAMS

Cotton canvas; wax resist, dip dyed; 32 by 33 inches.

A fanciful, playful gridwork of images—unlike those on TV.

G

Mary Ann Smith Boles

IRIS GRIDS #5-#7

Painted and dyed cotton canvas with trapunto quilting; 36 by 110 inches.

A

B

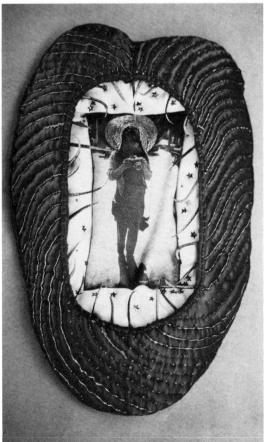

112

C

D

E

F

G

G

A
Roxanne Kukuk
ONE LONELY HEART, ALL
TORN UP
Cotton, cotton blends,
nylon; wax resist
discharge and machine
applique; 18 by 18 inches.

B
Carol L. Baker
FOUR CORNERS
Screen printed cotton
sateen with a resist
stencil and pigment dye;
hand quilted center and
machine quilted and torn
paper frame; 58 by 57
inches.

C
Arnelle A. Dow
FEMININE MYSTIQUE
Batik on linen with direct
application of Procion
dyes; 32 by 42 inches.

A

B

C

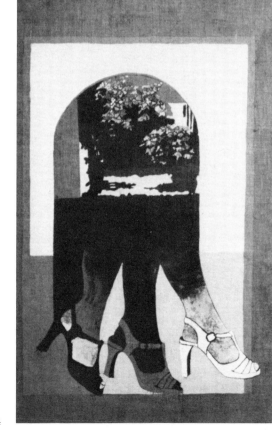

D
Dorte Christjansen
BIRCHES
Wax resist with protein dyes on Honan silk; 7 by 6½ feet.

D

E
Susanna Kuo
SQUARE SAIL
Katazome (stencil resist dyeing) on cotton organdy with turkey quills; 18 by 18 by 3 inches.

I am interested in the geometric and rhythmic basis of repeat patterns. This design is a synthesis of two kinds of structures: the organic form and fluid geometry of quills and the more rigid framework underlying man-made airfoils and winnowing devices such as sails, kites, gliders and fans.

D

E

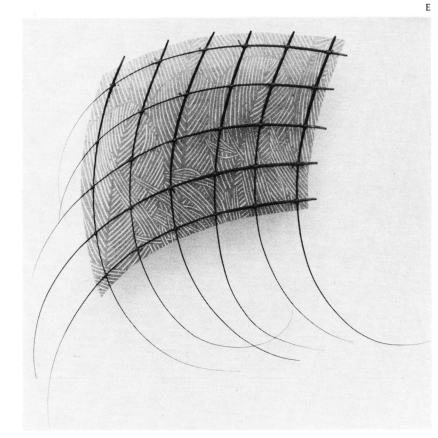

Robin Becker
I FELL INTO A DREAM
Color Xerox on silk and
satin, embedded into
paper; 21 by 21 inches.

B
Patricia L. Brown
BOXED SKIES
Direct application of
Procion dyes to cotton
velveteen, with applique
and machine quilting; 50
by 45 inches.

C
Naomi Kark Schedl
EPHEMERAL BLANKET II
Papercord, nylon mono-
filament, watercolor
paper, rice paper; 46 by
36 by 3 inches.

D
Kriss Jana Olsen
CITY WALL
Wool plain weave,
colored with pastels; 48
by 48 inches.

E
Bernita Dodge
SPRING MORNING
Batik on rayon and pongee silk; layered and hand quilted; 22 by 30 inches.

F
Sally Naftzinger
UNTITLED
Hand stitched and quilted muslin, painted with acrylics; 26 by 28 inches.

G
Carolyn Mason Ferrell
TRAPUNTO DRAWING
Colored pencil on canvas with trapunto; 5½ by 6½ feet.

H
Leslie A. Heckman
NO. 2 SILK CHIPS
Gutta resist dyed silk; 18 by 33 inches.

E

F

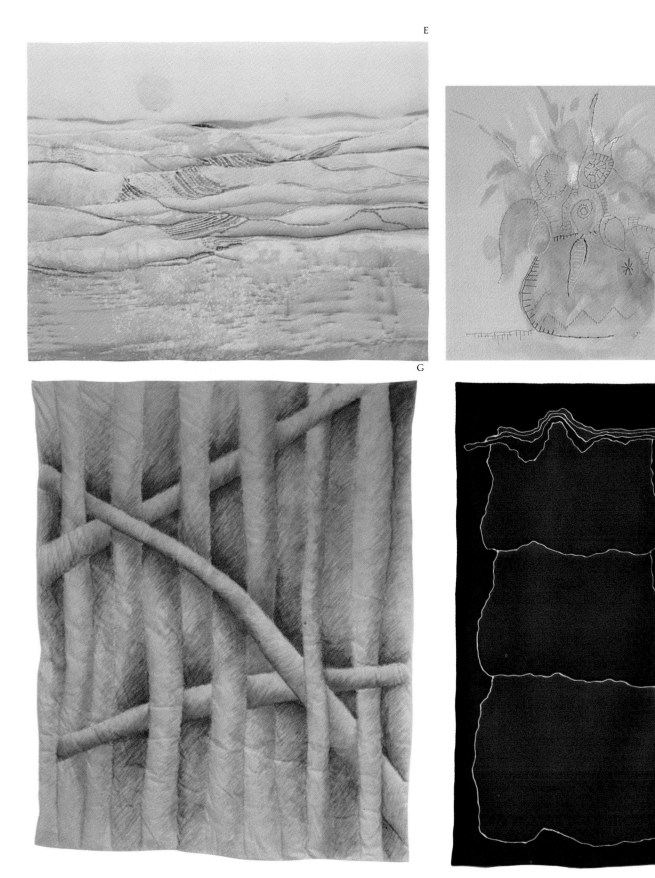

G

H

117

A

Kathleen Knippel
MELON VENDOR
Batik with Inko dyes on
cotton; quilting, trapunto,
applique; 17 by 22 inches.
This is one of eight batiked
pictures that will form a
photo-album-page quilt.

B

Richard Daehnert
IMAGE BANNER C. 1900
Photo-screen print on
canvas; 44 by 63 by 11
inches.

A

A

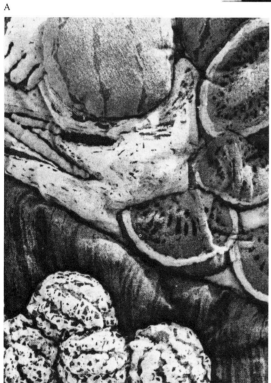

B

C

Ellen J. Zahorec
THREE X-RATED PILLOWS
Heat transfer and
stitchery on handmade
paper and fabric; 20 by
22 by 2 inches each.

*I am disillusioned, but
hopeful—romantic. Memory
and emotion give shape to
works that pull fragments of
the past into contemporary
precious objects.*

C

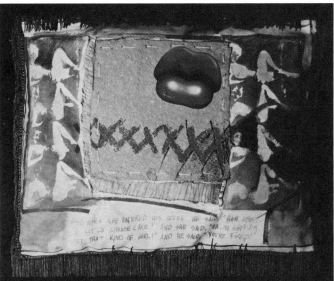

*And when she entered his
office, he said, "How about a
little cheesecake!" And she
said, "Oh, no sir! I'm not that
kind of girl!" And he said,
"You're fired!"*

C

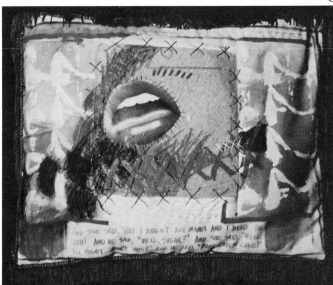

*And she said, "But I haven't
any money and I need the
job!" And he said, "Well,
Sugar?" And she said, "Well
all right. How's this?" And he
said, "More cheesecake!"*

C

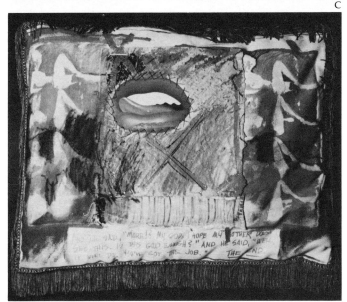

*And she said, "More?! My
God, I hope my Mother
doesn't see this. Is this good
enough?" And he said, "Well,
it will do. You've got the job."
The End.*

A

Victoria Z. Rivers
SELF PORTRAIT FANTASY I
Silk-screened and hand painted velveteen using Procion dyes; hand quilted and appliqued; 39 by 35 inches.

This work has to do with the moment that wishes and daydreams collide—with knowing the difference between wishes and fantasies, setting goals and priorities and trying to reach for the unobtainable.

B

Susan Aaron-Taylor
UNTITLED
Hand painted batik on rayon; 14 by 19 inches.

C

Bo Ball
THREE BIRDS IN FLIGHT
Batik and hand painting on satin and cotton sateen with Procion dye, India ink; 16 by 16 by 2 inches each.

D

Gloria Marconi
OVERLOADED SOCKET
Unbleached muslin; trapunto, hand quilting; airbrushed with dye; 11½ by 20¾ inches.
I just love feet!

E

Jane Thomas
TRIPTYCH: ENLISTMENT, ACTION, RETURNED
Found objects; contact-printed fabrics, using a line negative and Inko dye; hand and machine embroidery; 16 by 18 by 5 inches each.
The portrait contained in these shadow boxes is of my Great Uncle, who served in the First World War. This work is intended to remind people of the very personal effects of war—hopefully serving as a warning to help avoid repetition.

F

Blanche Cybele Derby
MOLA CAT SHIRT
Silk-screened cotton.

A

B

C

D

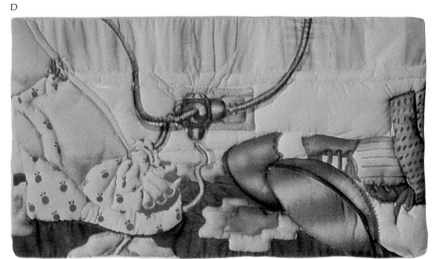

Patty Haag
EATING MAN'S HABIT
Quilted cyanotype; 23 by
19 inches.

H
Maria Lane O'Keefe
GINGERBREAD PEOPLE
Magic Marker on fabric;
clay faces painted with
oils; naturally dyed fleece
hair; 9 dolls—9 by 22 by
4 inches each.

*When I was a child, I would
draw all day, visiting these
people at the end of my pencil.
I believed it was only me (and
that pencil) who could bring
them into this world. I still
have this feeling when I finish
a doll.*

I
Beverly Rusoff
AFTER BLUE VELVET THRIFT
SHOP SPECIAL
Color Xerox on
handmade paper; hand
sewn with silk thread;
12½ by 14½ inches.

*Just before the battle Mother
I am thinking most of you
While upon the field we're lying
With the enemy in view.*

*He answered his country's call of
righteous cause, etc. "I was in France
about a week before I was into action
but I couldn't get into action quick
enough."*

*Buckingham Palace 1918—
The Queen and I wish you God-speed,
a safe return to the happiness and joy
of home life with an early restoration
to health. A grateful Mother country
thanks you for faithful services.
George R. 2*

E

F

H

G

I

A
Jessica Scarborough
EARTH BATIK II
Cotton; 14 by 17 inches.

The design is waxed on the fabric, and food (baby food, etc.) is applied to some areas of the design. This encourages mold growth and other interesting changes. The piece is then placed outdoors for a period of one to six months, then washed, ironed and framed.

B
Dorte Christjansen
ODE TO PACHELBEL
Wax resist with protein dyes on silk satin; 30 by 36 inches.

In order to convey, rather than copy, the beauty of nature, I combine images into a composite—the essence of what I see, remember and feel.

C
Rees Shearer
MR. JAMES
Batik with Procion dyes on cotton; 20 by 26 inches.

Mr. James was a simple, slight, strong-willed, mountain man who believed in sharing his time and skills with anyone who needed them. Although I never knew my natural grandfather, I and many others feel blessed to have known, loved and been loved by this adopted grandad who we all called "Mr. James."

A

B

C

D

James Nordmeyer
UNTITLED
Traditional batik on canvas, using Procion dyes; 25 by 32 inches.
This is a commissioned work! A gentleman brought me an old, torn photograph of his grandfather and friends, and wanted it translated into batik.

E

Lenore Davis
SHEET VII FLYING ACROBATS
Cotton sheet, brushed with thickened dye; 86 by 102 inches.
This is a multi-purpose sheet—to be used as a wall hanging, bed cover, ceiling piece, room divider, etc.

F

Sher Elkin
LADY I
Batik on cotton muslin; 27 by 41 inches.
The outlines and most of the painted areas were done with waterproof India inks. I used melted crayons to paint the face.

D

E

F

A
Patty Haag
CANADIAN POSTCARD #1
Painting on fabric; 29 by
44 inches.

B
Connie Ellis
FIGURES OF DESIRE
Direct dye batik on
cotton muslin with
Procion and Naphthal
dyes; 72 by 36 inches.

C
Ann Welch
CAEDMON'S SONG
Wax resist batik on silk;
61 by 41 inches.
*In this piece, every color and
form on the silk was produced
by full-immersion of the whole
cloth in a series of ten dye
baths, most of the colors being
executed by overlay of one
another—the dyes are never
painted on.*

*Whether on countless lakes or, three oceans....The Officer of the Royal Canadian Mounted Police
Symbolizes The Strength and Unity of CANADA.*

A

A

B

B

C

C

124

MINIATURES

overleaf
Gabriella Farkas
CONTRASTS
Stretched knitting of silk
and wool; 8 by 8 by 8
inches.

A
Pat Brown
NOVEMBER NOTES—
BUNDLED
Handmade paper of
tussah silk and sisal with
gold kimono thread;
Plexiglas base; 8 by 6½
by 10 inches.

B
Kathleen Knippel
MY KITCHEN WINDOW—
WITH GARDEN VIEW
Woven wool, linen and
nylon mesh, assembled
from 20 separate
sections;
8 by 8 by 2 inches.

*The window and shutters
open and close to reveal a
view of my garden. This
piece is a continuation of
my interest in soft
sculpture, and my wish to
depict the various things I
find of interest in the
wonderful Italian environment that I live in and love
so much.*

A

B

B

B

B

C

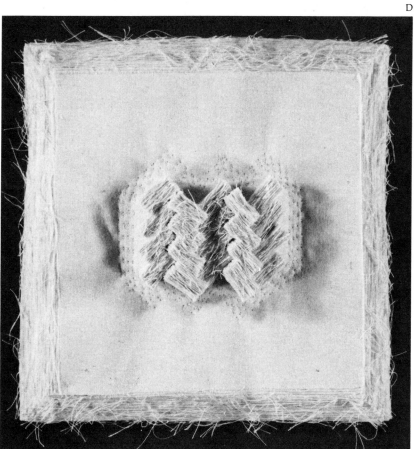

D

C
Kathleen Knippel
SOFT PHOTOS WITH
ENVELOPE: POULTRY MARKET
AND FISH MARKET
Batik with Inko dyes on
cotton; quilting, trapunto,
applique; envelope—8 by
5½ inches, photos—5½
by 5½ inches.

*I live next to the huge outdoor
market area of Florence, Italy,
and have taken hundreds of
photos of the market and small
shops in the area. This piece is
taken from some of those
photos.*

D
Ruth Geneslaw
MUSLIN SERIES: TWILL
Muslin; stacked, frayed,
turned on edge, hand-
stitched; 8 by 8 by 1½
inches.

*Observing a random stack of
muslin scraps in my studio, I
was drawn again and again to
the inherent beauty of the
frayed edges. I set about
cutting and arranging small
stacks of muslin into tight,
geometric configurations.
Thus, the muslin series was
born two years ago, conceived
only in miniature terms—they
are intended to be intimate and
to engage the viewer at close
range.*

E
Judith Crawford
UNTITLED
Knotted cotton netting,
Plexiglas, and wood; 6 by
9¾ by 4¾ inches.

*My interest is in line and
space, and in the grid
structures resulting from the
single-element technique of
knotted netting. By draping
and/or stretching the grids and
placing them on consecutive
planes, closed, dense areas and
open tunnels are created.*

E

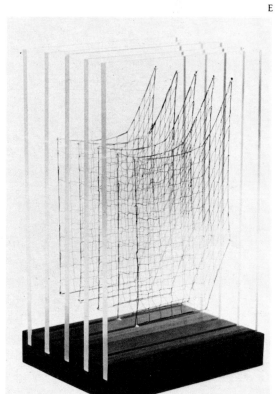

A
Patricia T. Hetzler
WOVEN PASTEL PAPER#2
Embroidered, torn and
woven handmade paper,
transfer printed with
disperse dyes, colored
pencils; 8 by 10 inches.
*I am trained as a painter, and
have been weaving for nine
years. However, during the
past 10 months I have been
working almost exclusively in
the area of handmade paper. I
am still weaving, but seem to
be moving back towards
painting—on weavings and
paper.*

B
Linda Catherine Coenen
MAGIC SQUARE
Satin stitch with cotton
embroidery floss; 8 by 8
inches.

C
Susan Hoover
UNTITLED TAPESTRY
Slit tapestry of silk and
metallic threads; 3¾ by
5½ inches.

D
Mary Bero Nechvatal
PHYSICAL GRAFFITO
Muslin, silk; fiber
reactive dyes; hand
stitched, applique; 9 by 9
inches.
*Source of inspiration? Cave
drawings and bathroom walls.*

A

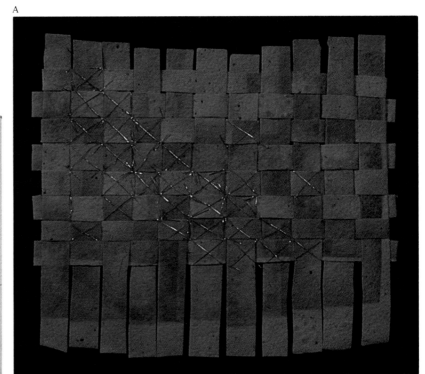

B

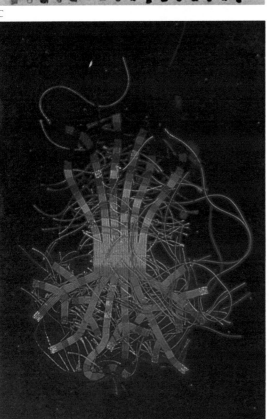

C

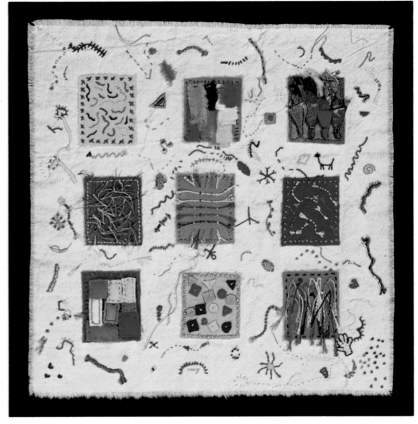

D

128

E

Cynthia A. Snellman
UNTITLED
Handmade paper formed
in a grease clay mold;
twigs bound with copper
wire with coiled ends; 4
by 4 by 5 inches.

F

Ann S. Coates
ONE OF OUR PLANETS IS
MISSING
Handmade paper of plain
and dyed cotton pulp;
laminated, stitched and
inscribed; 8 by 8 inches.

G

Susan Lindsay
MOTHERS
Linen, coconut grass;
stitched; 7½ by 5 by 1
inches.
*The forms that I create,
whether encased and
bound, or free and soaring
represent a personal
struggle which I feel is also
a universal one.*

H

Anne Dushanko-Dobek
SOUVENIR XXXIX
Fragments of letters,
photographs, cotton
thread, paper pulp; 5¼ by
7½ inches.
*This is one of 40 handmade
paper collages consisting of
found materials woven into a
warp of cotton threads, prior to
immersion in a vat of paper
pulp. These are memories of
remembrances, both in the
physical sense of tokens, and in
a psychological sense.*

E

F

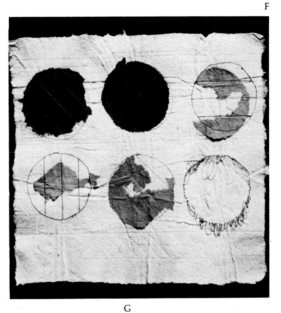

G

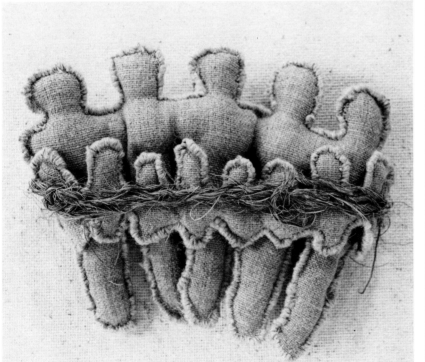

H

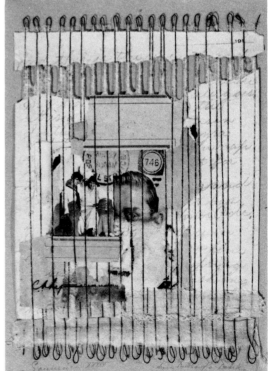

A
Anne McKenzie Nickolson
ZIG ZAG II
Embroidery on Procion-
dyed cotton rickrack;
pieced; 5¼ by 5 inches.

B
Susan Lange
SAND FAN
Handmade paper (flax,
chicory, cotton), threads,
sand; lamination of wet
fibers pulled on a screen;
10½ by 11½ inches.
Photo by Bob Barrett.
*Working with paper allows me
the freedom that I always
wanted when drawing on
paper . . . I am enchanted
with the malleability of a wet
sheet, and the strength of the
dry, but still fragile quality of
the sheet. Laminating layers of
colored pulp and storing secrets
within them is so like the
hidden beauty in the depths of
all of us.*

C
Hey Frey
COLLECTED MEMORIES
Tapestry weave and
felting with cotton, wool
flax and silk; 7 by 7½ by
1 inches.

D
Patricia Williams
STRUCTURED SURFACE 3
Crochet with rayon fiber;
10 by 12 inches.

A
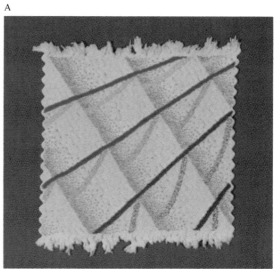

A
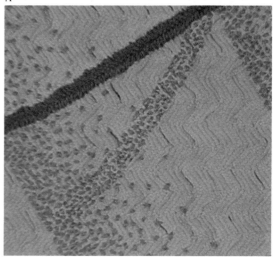

B

C

D
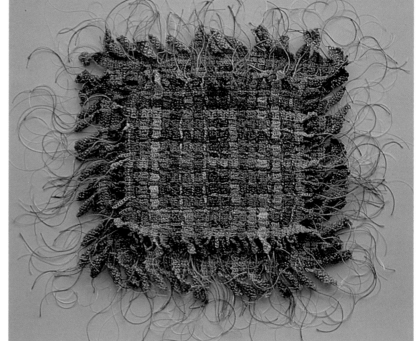

E
Elizabeth Fuller
ORANGE SECTION
Airbrushed and penciled
cotton organdy; 5 by 5 by
5 inches.

F
Sarah Redfield
RECYCLE MANIA #4
Old magazine ads,
snipped and pulped in a
blender; one of four
works, each 4 by 5
inches.
*We live in a world of
beautiful rubbish. If you are
an impoverished artist and
have trouble paying for
materials, always remember
that there is gold in your
wastebasket!*

G
Diane Itter
GREEN LATTICE
Knotted linen; 8 by 5½
inches.

E

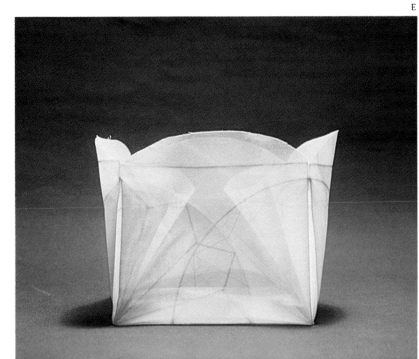

F

G

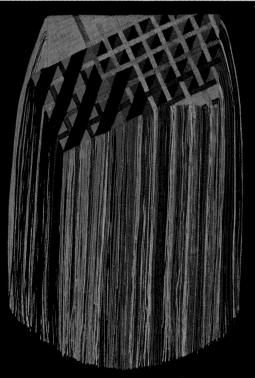

A

Shereen LaPlantz
UNTITLED
Twined and sewn round
reed, dried flowers,
bamboo leaves and palm
fibers; 12 by 7 inches.

B

Len Bentham
SOFT BOX WITH ASCENDING
AND DESCENDING STAIRS
Linen paper; 6 by 5 by 6
inches.
*I'm self-taught in basketry and
textiles and work mainly with
plaiting because of the clean-
ness of line obtainable. Last
year, a friend gave me some
ticker tape to experiment with,
and I began exploring the
interior space of the box form.
I have since stopped using
ticker tape and now use pure
white linen paper. I have also
reduced the scale by as much
as 75%.*

C

Sheila Benedis
BASKETRY BOWL 5
Diamond pattern
basketry with day lily
stems, reeds and dyed
maple bark; 9 by 5 by 9
inches.

A

B

C

Hisako Sekijima
MOSAIC III
Cherry bark, white birch
bark, dolacena frond and
rattan in a mosaic
weave—a combination of
wickerwork, twining and
overlaying; 10 by 8 by 10
inches. Photo by Bob
Hanson.

*Over the past ten years, I have
developed my own basketry
techniques, experimenting with
ancient, traditional and non-
traditional methods. Basketry
has become my "language" by
which I can express my
delight, my anger, my
attention and my concept of
value.*

E
Kimberly Mason
NOTIONS OF AUNT BERTHA,
REMNANTS OF A CULTURED
LADY
Coiling and embroidery
with cotton floss and
cord, linen, antique
buckles and buttons; 7 by
7 by 3 inches.

*Inspired by a woman who
surrounded herself with
beautiful things that have now
become family heirlooms.*

F
Mona Elise Rummel
FASCINATION
Wheat stitch with
Ponderosa pine needles
and raffia; 4½ by 5½
inches.

D

E

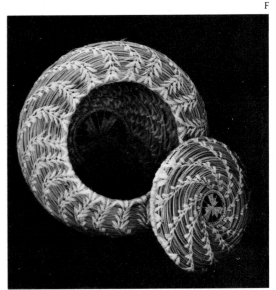

F

A
Virginia Davis
PERUVIAN PUMA REPEAT
Color Xerox and
stitchery on handwoven
silk; 8 by 8 by 1½ inches.
*I want to present fibers and
fabric structure with images
from a different angle, to evoke
a response from the viewer.*

C
Marjorie J. Rubin
ALLIGATORS ON AN
AFTERNOON ROMP
Handwoven cotton with
ironed-on color Xerox
transfers; 52 by 4 inches.

B
Patricia Wheeler
NAVAJO WEAVER V
Photo silk-screen and
warp painting on cotton;
9 by 12½ inches.
*I am working with integrating
the structure of the weave and
the design on the surface. My
inspiration is from Indian
weavers, and women of the
past who worked with textiles.*

A

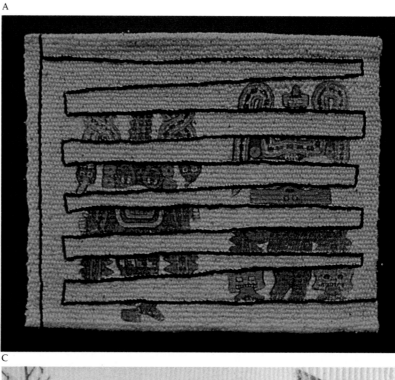

B

C

C

D
Peggy Moulton
MARBLE GAME FOR GIANT
SOFTIES
Felting, re-felting and
knotless netting with
wool, lint and yarns;
bag—10 by 12 inches,
marbles—7½ inch
circumference.

E
Joan Tomoff
BLUE LANDSCAPE
Rayon on cotton warp;
hand dyed yarn;
boundweave; 6 by 6
inches.

F
Kate Woolstenhulme
LANDSCAPE SERIES #7
Rayon; Deka and
Cushing dyes; painted
warp, multi-colored weft;
7½ by 6½ inches.
*I love being bold with color.
As does the misplaced flower
in a garden or field of
wildflowers, I allow the
unexpected bit of color to
enrich the already glowing
surface.*

D

E

F

F

A

Julia Rapinoe
CARVED BY THE RAIN
Wool on linen, slit
tapestry; 8 by 10 inches.

*Living in southern California,
I cannot help being influenced
by the erosion of her hillsides
and cliffs by the sea and the
rain.*

B

Marian Hill Garfolo
MOUNTAINS IN THE SKY
Silk tapestry; 8 by 8
inches.
*I am a "detail-ist"—I love to
create small worlds where one
must take time to explore.*

C

Karen Meyerhoff
HUMAN/LANDSCAPE FORM
#3
Cotton and linen; Theo
Moorman inlay; 5 by 7
inches.
*I want to convey a feeling of
sensuality without graphically
representing it. The intentional
ambiguity of the composition
suggests other, more public
connotations, such as
landscape.*

A

B

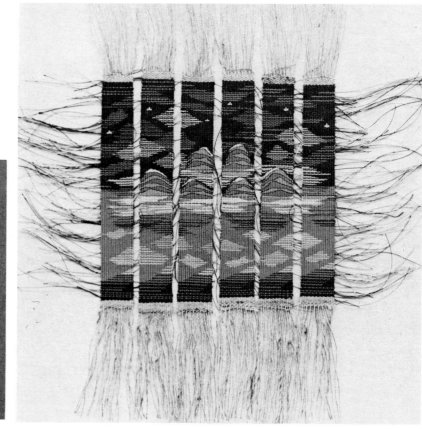

C

D

D

E

F

D
Norma Minkowitz
COME FORTH
Crocheted cotton over a
plastic egg shape; 4¾ by
6 by 6½ inches. Photo by
Bob Hanson.

E
Lesley E. Shearer
HOPE
Experimental multi-
harness weaving of hand
dyed wool and mohair,
mounted on a Plexiglas
base; 6 by 5 inches.
Photo by E. Ann Hunt.

F
Hey Frey
PRISM
Weaving and wrapping; 8
by 8 inches.

A
Lori Christmastree

KATHY (AND DEVORA)

Hand dyed silk on
handmade birch loom; 8
by 11 by 2 inches.

*I weave one of these tapestries
each summer, and they have a
different feeling from the rest
of my work. They really come
from a different part of my
personality. They started out
as self-portraits, but now are
portraying my friends.*

B
Linda V. Fiore

FRONT AND BACK

Cotton, wool and nylon,
tapestry weave with
surface embroidery; 5 by
7 inches.

C
Nancy Berry

HIGH HEELS

Aubusson tapestry of
Persian wool; 10 by 11
inches.

*I wanted the piece to have
something of the feeling of old,
yellowed family album
photographs. The shoes and
wallpaper are from the 40's,
and the carpet is from my
childhood memories of
Saturday afternoons in the
movie theater.*

D
Jane Feldblum

FARM

Knotted cotton and linen;
3¼ by 3¾ inches.

*I work on a small scale
because it is comfortable for
me, and also portable.*

A

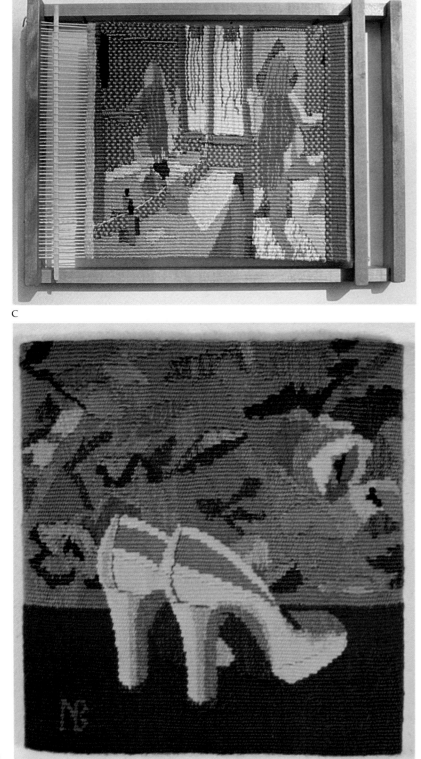

C

B

D

138

WEARABLES

A

overleaf
Julia Hill
KIMONO FOR A SPRING
FESTIVAL
Siamese silk; watercolor
technique, resist, third
layer of batik. Photo by
Tohru Nakamura.

A
Candiss Ann Cole
LENO DRESS
Leno weave of 100%
viscose, with Danish
medallion accents at
neckline, bodice and hem.
Photo by Don Sparks.

B

B
Patricia Wheeler
TRANSPARENT NIGHTGOWN
Photo silk-screen of a
pattern weave on silk and
rayon.

C
Jim Carr
UNTITLED
CUM cotolin; tabby
weave, mock leno.

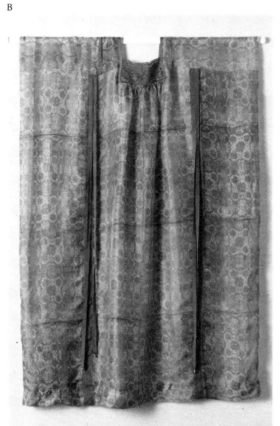

C

D

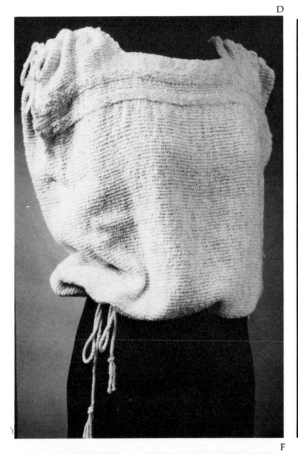

E

Myra Reichel
BLOUSON
Handwoven cotton,
shaped on the loom with
double weave casings and
borders.

E

Joy W. Saville
SEMINOLE NOMAD DRESS
Voile, crinkle cotton,
satin ribbon; Seminole
patchwork.

*When I wear this dress, I
want to run through the hills
barefoot!*

F

Maria da Conceicao
CAPE AND HAT
Pure silks, hand stitched
with silk thread. Photo
by Jamie Phillips.

F

F

A

Elsie Blaschke
COAT FOR A BUTTERFLY
HUNTER
Reverse applique and
stitchery with silk thread
and silk fabric.

B

Dona Dowling Abt
PAINTED DRESS
Fiber reactive dyes,
metallic thread and rayon
challis.

*The dress is made of a number
of rectangles, each painted
separately before construction.*

C

Crane Day
DISCO DRESS
Rayon, tabby weave; size 5.

*This was an exciting project
because the design of the dress
"happened" as I cut the warp
from the warping reel. The
"tassel" quality of the rayon
and the drape cried out to be
captured in this design. All
this took place while I was
actually searching for a
suitable weight synthetic for
summer stoles.*

D

Candiss Ann Cole
IKAT DRESS
Ikat on handwoven silk,
with antique glass
buttons down the back of
dress. Photo by Don
Sparks.

*The back of this dress has
several darts around the
neckline which create a blouson
effect to the waistline.*

A

B

C

D

142

E

F

E
Sandi Wright
EARTH AND SAGE
Silk, hand dyed cotton
and chenille. Photo by
Dick Faller.

F
Dione Christensen
SWEATER AND SKIRT
Handknit wool sweater;
cotton skirt with textile
paint. Photo by Allan
Tannenbaum.

G
Ann Marie Patterson
M & M FRUIT SALAD
Rayon chiffon, hand
painted with water color
wash and Procion dyes.

*By adding water to dye or
pigments, I can achieve
overlays and transparencies.
The addition of various pastes
in combination with the dyes
creates a hard edge. If I desire
a soft fuzzy edge, I paint dye
next to cassava paste, and the
dye fuzzes as it flows into the
paste. Sometimes I wet the
fabric with a water-loaded
sponge, load a brush with dye
and paint over the wet fabric.
I watch the spreading dye and
work quickly to flood an area
with more water for
transparency. This gives a
very lucious wet-on-wet effect.*

G

H

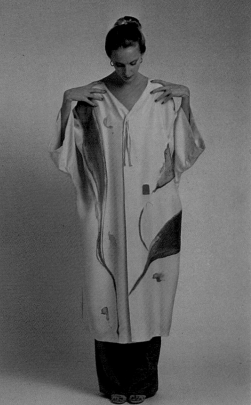

H
Cedrus Monte
UNTITLED
Direct application of fiber
reactive dye on silk.
Photo by Elaine Keenan.

*I see clothing as a mask that
has the potential to transform
the spirit of the psyche.
Clothing can allow the wearer
to take part in an alchemical
transformation using texture,
form, color, mood and
movement. When I design the
actual garment, I keep in mind
the fluidity and grace of the
body, keeping the elements of
mystery and magic ever-
present.*

A
Cristie Thomas
UNTITLED
Hand dyed and natural,
pure wild silk; tabby
weave with pulled weft.

B
**Pamela Gibson
Schoenborn**
KIMONO
Handspun silk with warp
ikat.

C
Lynn Hazelton
UNTITLED
Woven cotton with
kasuri (ikat) techniques;
52 by 58 inches.

*In this piece I have used
various Japanese kasuri
techniques. Besides the
standard wrapping for resist
dyeing, I am also using a
technique called Bokashi
Gasuri. The warp is braided
before dyeing to achieve the
mottled effects of the
background colors . . .*

A

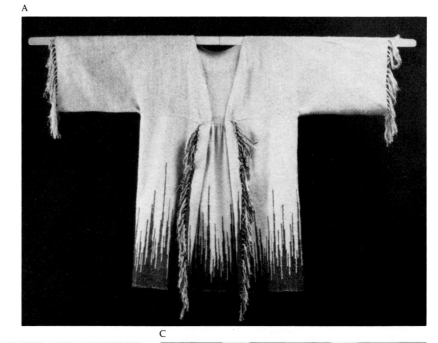

B

C

C

B

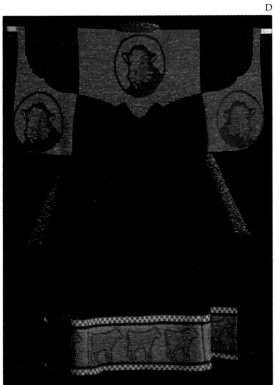

D

E

F

G

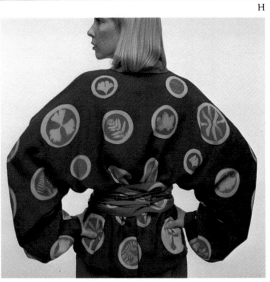

H

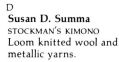

D
Susan D. Summa
STOCKMAN'S KIMONO
Loom knitted wool and
metallic yarns.

E
Jane Lang Axtell
JAPANESE DOFUKO
Seminole patchwork with
cotton and silk; 52 by 48
(extended sleeves) inches.
*Clothing is my form of
individual expression,
combining aesthetics and
function.*

F
Melissa J. Brown
FLYING GEESE KIMONO
Handwoven, reversible
fabric of natural cotton
and novelty slub with
silk-screen printed warp.
Handsewn kimono; fabric
width 13½ inches. Photo
by David Gaynes.

G H
Danica Eskind
EVENING JACKET—HIPPARI
Photograms on rayon
challis using single
application and exposure
of photo-sensitive Inko
dye, plus a final Procion
over-dye. Photo by Jim
Charles.

A

Norma Minkowitz

UNTITLED

Knitted and crocheted
cotton.

*Wearables have become very
special to me in the past few
years. As a child, I crocheted
clothing right onto my dolls—
it was wearable sculpture. I
feel the same way now. Each
piece is a unique, sculptural
adventure.*

B

Therese Y. Zemlin

SHAWL—COAT

Plain woven wool and
mohair, fabric, pleated
and sewn, with crocheted
neckline.

*This is a revised version of the
Vogue cocoon wrap, generally
re-worked to suit custom-
designed, loosely-woven wool.
The Vogue design is probably
a takeoff on the 1920's
butterfly dresses, and I feel I've
made enough of a change to
call the design (including color
and choice of materials) mine.
If in doubt, see Vogue Pattern
#7233!*

A

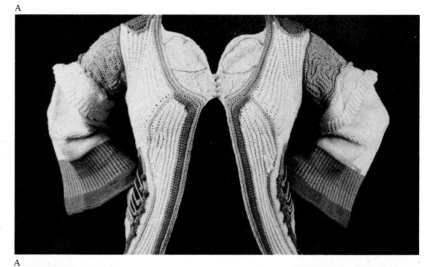

A

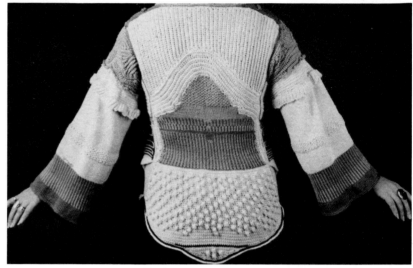

B

B

C

Debi Sunderman
MARSHMALLOW DOUBLET
Stuffed, double woven
wool, lined with rayon
satin.

D

Molly Ireland
GUINEA FEATHER COAT
Handspun wool, ikat
warp using Ciba dyes;
lining of batiked silk,
using Procion dyes.

*This pattern was adapted from
a Turkestan silk ikat robe.
The feather motif ikat design
was inspired by my pair of
guineas. The silk lining is an
abstraction of the guinea
feather itself, which is very
beautiful and fanciful.*

E

Maralyce Ferree
FREE IMPACT
Woven lightweight CUM
wool with ikat.

*My weavings are dual-
functioning; they may be
displayed on the wall when not
being worn.*

F

Ellen Hirshberg
COAT
Silk; warp painted on
loom with Procion dyes.

147

A
Pamela Eve Brazier
MANIFESTO VESTO
Appliqued satins and colored lame. Photo by Laura Schneider.

The portraits of Marx, Engels, Stalin, Mao and Chou En Lai are jacquard weavings imported from Red China.

B
Mimi Rondenet
UNTITLED
Machine quilted and appliqued cotton and rayon.

C
Pat Richardson
SHADOW WEAVE CAPE III
Wool, shadow weave; 130 inches wide.

I enjoy developing unusual pattern weaves which create additional patterns when the fabric is cut and assembled. This seems to make the final piece more exciting. It's like creating a complex puzzle, planning the fabric and how each part of it will interlock precisely with another.

D
Pamella Saffer
SERAPE
Warp faced ikat of angora, wool and nylon blends; 34 by 72 inches.

E
Mathilde Salomon
QUEBEC
Crocheted wool rug yarns and assorted remnants. Photo by Daniel E. Quat.

The patchwork approach in collage, quilting and stained glass work appeals to me and lends itself to crochet.

F
Elizabeth Coleman
GEOMETRIC SMOCK
Appliqued cotton, hand and machine stitched. Photo by Paul Brandwein.

I cut most of my patterns from geometric shapes. Squares and rectangles lend themselves easily to the human form and can be modified with gathering or smocking—sometimes they're fine the way they are.

A

A

B

C

D

G

G
Cate Fitt
LA FRIVOLITE
Hand quilted silk,
airbrushed and hand
painted with fiber
reactive dyes.

*"La Frivolite" is the French
word for tatting.*

H
James Williams
INFASHIA
Wool needlepoint on
front and side panels;
1920's quilt pieces in
back.

E

F

G

G

H

149

A

Barbara Beccio-Ratches
FULL MOON COAT
Applique and quilting
with cotton velveteen
and metallic thread.

B

Judy Branfman
ROSE VEST
Wool, mohair, linen,
hand dyed and handspun
yarns, satin lining,
porcelain buttons; warp
brocade patterning with
honeycomb cloth.

C

Jane Lang Axtell
JAPANESE DOFUKO
Seminole patchwork with
cotton and silk.

D

North Country Textiles
LONG HEATHER TABARD
Wool and cotton,
handwoven twill with
twill inlay. Photo by
Anne Elzas-O'Keefe.

*North Country Textiles is a
partnership of five
designer/weavers: Georgia
Beatty, Sheila Denny-Brown,
Ron King, Carole Ann Larson
and June Sproule. It was
founded in 1976 and has since
been producing a new line of
fine handwoven clothing each
year. Members collaborate on
the original designs and
fabrics, run the business and
weave the cloth.*

A

B

C

D

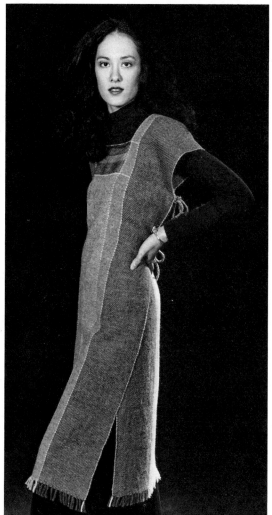

150

E
Brenda Colling
STREETSCAPE
Machine pieced, quilted, appliqued, embroidered wool with cotton padding.
This is a graphic of my terrain as I cycle through the city of Toronto.

F
Marian Clayden
CHENILLE COAT
Clamp resist dyed cotton chenille.

E

E

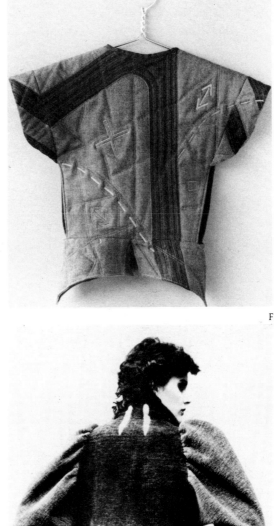

F

F

A

Sharon Robinson
GLADDY'S NEW CLOTHES
Horse blanket; transfer-
printed and disperse-dyed
nylon, pieced and quilted;
8 by 6½ feet.

B

Robyn Jennings
TROPICAL SUMARI
Mohair metallic; plain
weave; 56 by 35 inches.

*I love the tropics. A lot of my
work is inspired by tropical
flowers; i.e., orchids, plumeria,
fuchsias.*

C

Janet Higgins
STAR VEST
Machine quilted satin and
silk with metallic threads,
sequins and rhinestones.
Photo by Alan Loveless.

*I felt very ambivalent about
the clothing I make for a long
time—feeling it wasn't as
important as the wall
hangings I do. But I've come
to realize that the clothes may
have an even richer existence—
they can go out into the world,
rather than just hanging on
the wall. I view the clothing
that I do as sculpture, and
hope that the pieces will be
hung on the wall, instead of in
the closet, when they're not
being worn!*

D

Elizabeth Coleman
MAGIC SHOES
Reverse applique of
cotton and suede;
embroidery, hand and
machine stitching with
cotton and metallic
thread. Photo by Alan
Zaretsky.

*My mother had a direct
influence on my early work.
She used to buy me sets of pre-
stamped pillow cases to
embroider for relatives who
were getting married. This
was my first experience with
the creative flow vs. the
deadline.*

E

Geraldine Serpa
SILK AND SATIN
Silk, satin and beads;
7 by 10 inches.

A

B

A

C

C

D

F
Ruth Bilowus
COLLAR NECKLACE
Pearl cotton, silver, tapestry.

G
Susanna E. Lewis
OZ SOCKS
Machine knit wool, cotton, rayon and metallic yarn with satin fabric; beads and heels; crochet outline; shoe, sock and leg knitted as one piece; 36 inches long.
The right leg is Kansas and the left leg Oz!

E

F

G

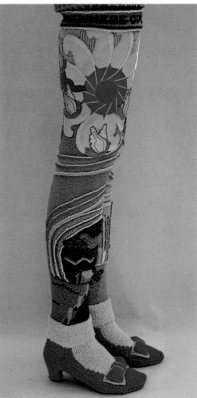

G

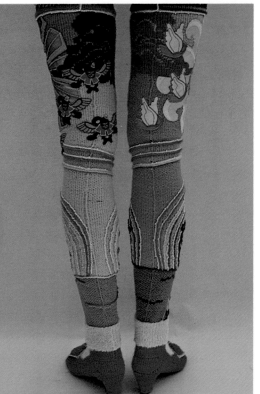

G

153

A
Mary Ann Clayton
NECKPIECE
Wool on silk tapestry
technique; coiling—silk
over wire; 9 by 16 inches.

B
Susanna E. Lewis
AT NIGHT ALL CATS ARE
GRAY
Machine knit wool, rayon
and metallic yarn with
satin fabric applique;
diameter—8 feet,
length—47 inches.

C
Tina Johnson-DePuy
WHITE SHELL AND SUNRISE
Abalone; acrylic medium;
knotted, wrapped, sewn.
Photo by Richard Byrd.

D
Gammy Miller
ACCRETION
Waxed linens, half-
hitched around a clam
shell shard; length—23
inches, 3 inches across
the bottom.
*I am particularly drawn to
fragments, marked by time and
weather, and to the mystery of
putting things together again
in a different way, to create a
new whole.*

154

DIVERSIONS

Carol Hunter
LUCIANO
Quilt and old clothing
scraps, flax, wood; hand
and machine stitching;
assembled over central
dowel rod; 28 inches
high.

*The style of my work, and
methods I employ, have
developed as a result of my
respect for the primitive or folk
artist. I strive for a simple,
direct, "naive" expression,
combined with the essential
qualities of design and
craftsmanship.*

A
Deborah Bewley
GOING CRACKERS
Painted canvas; machine
quilted animals; box—35
by 12 by 19 inches.

B
Sarah Redfield
TUFFY
Knitted plastic strapping;
44 by 30 by 48 inches.

*I have always been charmed by
the form of little "plastic wool"
pot-scrubbers—the old ones
had the trade name TUFFY.
When I discovered the existence
of red and yellow plastic
strapping, I realized I could
make myself a nice, BIG one!*

C
Margaret Greger
RAINBOW LOG CABIN
Synthetic fabrics, cut and
fused with a hot knife,
mounted on a nylon
organdy backing; birch
dowels; 27 by 27 inches
with streamers—15 feet
each.

*My experiments in using a
stained glass effect for fabric
kites have progressed into
working with various quilt
patterns. I teach kite-making,
and my latest writing project
is the "how-tos" of fabric kites.*

D
Jo-Ellen Trilling
THE DEVIL'S PIGS
Silk, polyester, wool and
satin; beads, paint; 12 by
20 by 12 inches. Photo by
Bob Hanson.

E
Ann-Marie Gillett
PIGFIELD FOLLIES
Batik and trapunto with
black cotton; Procion
dyes, diluted bleach; 43
by 28 inches.

*Humor seems to sneak into a
lot of my work—probably a
reflection of my belief that
laughter is song!*

F
Ann Kronenberg
LOVE FOR THREE ORANGES
Crocheted cotton, acrylic,
wool and lame, quilted
and stuffed on a canvas
backing; 18 by 18 by ¾
inches.

A

B

C

D

E

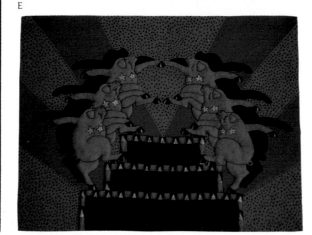

Annie Dempsey

A BIRD IN HAND
Crocheted silk, wool and
cotton with pipe cleaners;
15 by 16 by 9 inches.

H

F

Teresa Nomura

PIZZA WITH THE WORKS
Velvet, satin, chintz,
buttons, beads; 13 inches
in diameter, 1½ inches
high.

*This was commissioned for a
wedding present to a pair of
pizza fans!*

I

Barbara Bickell

BUDGIE
Silk fabric, painted with
acrylics; 6 by 9 by 6
inches.

*I would like to rekindle the
magic of childhood. Deep
inside, we still know we can
transform ourselves in the
twinkling of an eye!*

J

**Marilyn Lawrance
Harrison**

HOLD THE ONIONS
Cotton, silk; twill, velvet,
challis and satin fabrics
with a rayon base;
Procion and Inko dyes; 16
by 31 by 28 inches.

*Everytime I do a soft sculpture,
I swear never to touch another
curved needle. However, the
challenge of Wendicorp's
"Hot'n'Juicy Competition" was
too much. And I won!*

G

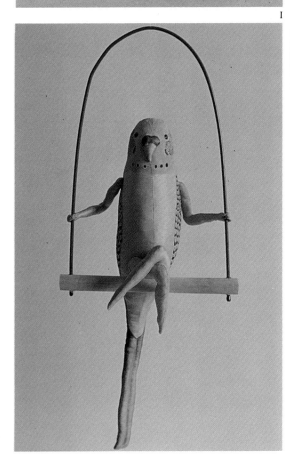

I

H

I

157

A
Lyn Carter
PIGALLE
Silk-screened, hand and
machine stitched cotton;
42 by 42 by 2 inches.

*I am specifically interested in
the contrast inherent in a soft
object with a mechanical form.
After buying a box of
marzipan pigs in separate
compartments, as a present for
a friend, I got the idea of
making my own soft sculpture
compartments that stuffed pigs
could snugly fit into.*

B
Denise Brunkus
MAURICE
Cotton muslin colored
with Crayolas and
marker, stuffed with rice;
machine and hand
embroidery and quilting;
15 by 16 by 5 inches.

*An illustrator by profession, I
bring my characters beyond the
realm of "flat". I am intrigued
with transposing my drawing
into something I can hold and
touch—to shake hands with
my drawings!*

A

B

B

C

Marjorie Graham Trout
CLOSELY WOVEN FAMILY
Velour, panne and acrylic fabrics; 16 elements designed and constructed separately, then woven together; 33 by 31 by 5 inches. Photo by Buchner and Young.

My work has evolved from strong interests in drawing, sculptural ceramics, weaving and the fiber arts. Soft sculpture allows me to combine the best of each media and mix in a little humor.

D

Lenore Davis
PAIR OF GNOME ACROBATS
Machine stitched cotton and velveteen, brushed and stamped with unthickened fiber reactive dyes; 15 by 16 by 5 inches.

E

Shelly Gladstone-Fowler
THE EMBRACE
Quilting, applique, embroidery with cotton and silk; figures designed to hang on the wall; 14 by 23 inches.

D

E

A

Noreen Crone-Findlay
LADY GODIVA
Hand stitched cotton; 28 by 30½ inches.

LADY GODIVA and I spent three tumultuous years together. Because of the slow and gentle pace of working the hand embroidery, she was a tremendous source of solace to me. We went through many transformations together.

B

Renie Breskin Adams
LET'S BE CIVILIZED
Cotton; looped embroidery stitch with couching, satin stitch and needleweaving; 13½ by 17½ inches.

This is my execution of an assignment I gave my students—to construct an image/object which aesthetically incorporates something found in their environment. This antique wooden frame served as my "embroidery hoop", and inspiration for the development of form and content.

C

Renie Breskin Adams
FEAR, LAUGHTER AND THE UNKNOWN
Cotton; looped embroidery stitch with satin stitch, chain stitch, couching and needle-weaving; 24 by 30 inches.

This was constructed over a period of 13 months. It represents a major development in my studio work, in terms of integrating formal ideas about color and rhythm in prior "abstract" images with literary or representational ideas and meanings.

A

B

C

C

D

D
Nancy Camden Hauser
COUNTRY COUPLE
Cotton and other natural
fabrics, hand em-
broidered and quilted;
designed to hang on a
wall; 31 by 18 by 9
inches.

The COUNTRY COUPLE *grew
from a love of old family
photographs taken in the
1930's and 1940's, and
memories of the older, Indiana
farmers and their wives.*

E
Ann Watson
TIME OUT
Velveteen, denim, cotton,
satin, wool; embroidered
face; painted pretzels,
beer can and TV guide;
36 by 14 by 22 inches.
Photo by Joe A. Watson.

E

E

161

A

Shelly Gladstone-Fowler
GREEN BOX
Quilting, applique and
embroidery with cotton,
silk; 4 by 4 inches.

*I believe that there is little
difference between fantasy and
reality. (A psychiatrist once
told me that this was my
major problem!) When we look
through the window of art,
into a different place or level,
the new place becomes part of
our own personal environment.
I hope my work helps people
play into a larger picture of
life that will help expand the
imagination.*

B

Susan Morrison
SUGAR DADDY
Stuffed, sewn fabric; 14
inches high.

*My work is about humorous,
fun and simple moments in
time and space, and of our
relationships to others.*

C

Benita Cullinan
OOO LA LA
Embroidery on velveteen
and satin with feathers;
30 by 40 inches.

*I like people to have a good
time looking at my work!*

A

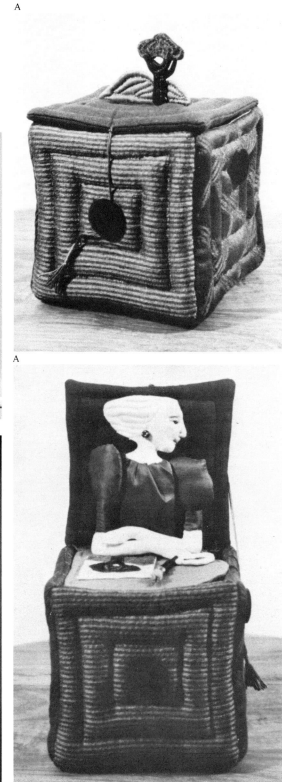

A

B

C

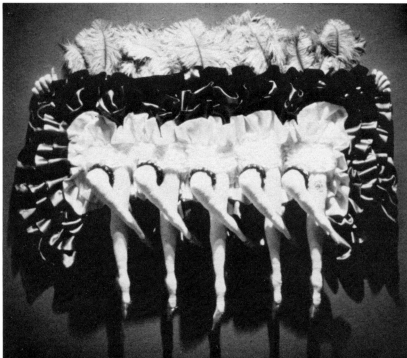

D
Judith Hawk
SWEATER FOR KING KONG
Crocheted wool and
cotton; 6 by 10 feet.
Photo by Matt Silver-
man.

E
Cynthia Kurkowski
PORTABLES
Various fabrics and vinyl;
silk-screening process; 15
by 11 by 7 inches.

F
Cynthia Kurkowski
DEE DEE'S TOP TEN
Various fabrics, sequins,
glitter; acrylic paints; 15
by 10 by 20 inches.

D

E

F

163

A
Margaret Greger
AIR MAIL KITE
Synthetic, outdoor-wear
material, birch dowels;
Seminole quilted border;
31 by 23 inches and three
streamers attached—15
feet each.

*Another visual pun, one in a
series of letters exchanged by
Rufous Hummingbird, Rosy
Finch, Lark Bunting and
Rusty Blackbird.*

B
Betsy Sibley
SWALLOWS NEST
Felted wool, unspun flax,
dyed raffia and feathers;
5 by 4 inches.

C
Carol Eckert
UNTITLED
Coiled cotton; 7 by 8½
inches.

164

D
Jappie King Black
SIREN
Wrapped, crocheted and stitched cotton, wool, silk, linen, fiber rush and alpaca; 14 by 11 by 10 inches.

E
Linda Carollo Endres
WOVEN WOMEN
Wool on linen tapestry over mahogany plywood forms; 12 by 5 inches each.
These women represent different stages in my Grandmother's life.

D

E

E

A

Heather Alexander
JENNY'S HOUSE
Hand dyed and pre-dyed
cotton and velveteen,
with hand and machine
stitchery and quilting; 28
by 21 by 22 inches.

*This house is fashioned after
the doll house which appeared
in a recurring dream I had as
a child. The inside is quilted
and has handwoven rugs and
soft sculpture fireplaces.*

B

Louise Fischer
717 LEXINGTON
Versatex on cotton;
quilted; 30 by 40 inches.

*My goal is to make the viewer
smile.*

C

Alma Lesch
FAMILY PORTRAIT
Cotton and wool,
stitchery on a feed bag;
15 by 21 inches.

A

C

D

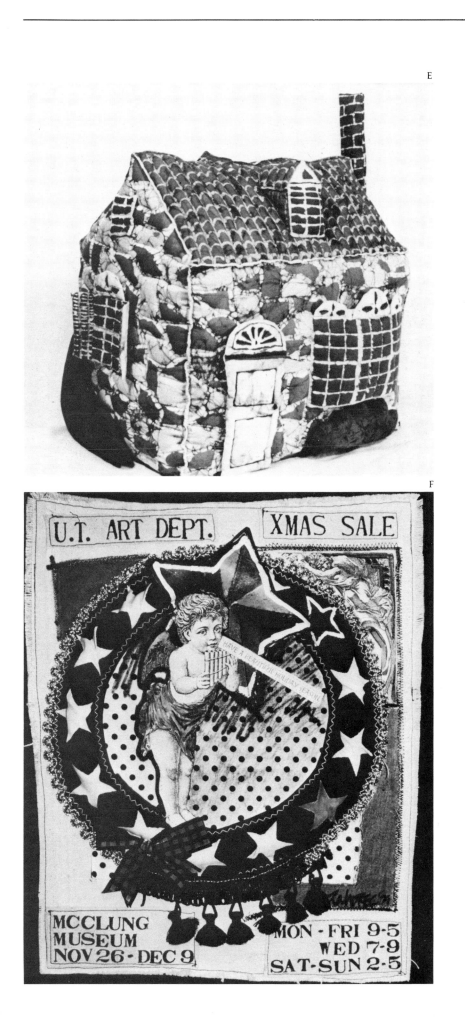

E

F

Margaret Mariner
ROOM PILLOW **#1**
Machine quilted muslin,
hand painted with Deka
permanent dye; 16 by 16
inches.

E

Christine Makowski
FULL HOUSE
Batik on cotton with
machine and hand
quilting; 18 by 18 by 12
inches.

F

Ellen J. Zahorec
CHRISTMAS POSTER
Drawing and stitchery on
paper, fabric; 12 by 16
inches.
*Nostalgic imagery is my
method for immortalizing
bygone times.*

A
Deborah Bewley
BALL AND JACKS
Vinyl and millium; ball—
11 inches in diameter,
jacks—16 by 17 by 17
inches.

*I work and experiment in
many fiber medias, but my
favorite is soft sculpture. I
enjoy taking everyday objects
and drawing attention to them.
I also enjoy watching people's
reactions to my work—they
laugh and have fun with it,
but I also hope they look at the
things around them in a new
light.*

B
Andrea V. Uravitch
THE YOUNG BUCK
Crocheted, woven and
stitched wool with wood,
steel, glass and foam
rubber; 21 by 63 by 67
inches. Photo by Joan
Marcus.

A

B

C

C
Dorothy Caldwell
BRIDES MASK
Wax resist with Indigo
and Procion dyes on
quilted cotton; 39 by 18
by 5 inches.

D
Carolyn Vosburg Hall
NINE CATS
Stuffed, sewn, appliqued,
embroidered and dyed
cotton, wool, velvet,
grass, linen and vinyl; 8
by 16 by 12 inches each.

*These are five from my series
of nine cats—an attempt to
express the essential nature of
cats I've owned or known.*

C

D

THE FIBERARTS DESIGN BOOK

Editor: **Kathleen DeBoy**

Art and Layout: Rob Pulleyn and Ann Uffelman

Valuable Advice: Richard Cain, Sally Hickerson-Hall,
Henry Johnson, John Kelsey, Jean Koefoed,
Jane Luddecke, Rich Mathews,
Kate Mathews-Pulleyn, Elaine Thompson,
Lynn Yarbrough

Technical Assistance: Paul Brezny, Robert Brown, John Hart,
Danny Lail, Robert Moore, Robert Mullinnix

Color Separations: Arts Engraving Co., Inc.

FIBERARTS MAGAZINE

Editor: Jane Luddecke

Publisher: Rob Pulleyn

Staff: Sally Hickerson-Hall, Jeane Hutchins,
Kate Mathews-Pulleyn, Elaine Thompson,
Ann Uffelman

INDEX